WISE WORDS & COUNTRY WAYS FOR COOKS

RUTH BINNEY

A DAVID & CHARLES BOOK

David & Charles is an F+W Publications Inc. company
4700 East Galbraith Road
Cincinnati, OH 45236

First published in the UK in 2008

A catalogue record for this book is available from the British Library.

ISBN-13: 978-0-7153-3008-1 hardback
ISBN-10: 0-7153-3008-X hardback

Printed in the UK by CPI William Clowes Beccles NR34 7TL
for David & Charles
Brunel House Newton Abbot Devon

Commissioning Editor: Neil Baber
Editorial Manager: Emily Pitcher
Desk Editor: Emily Rae
Art Editor: Sarah Clark
Designer: Sabine Eulau
Production Controller: Kelly Smith

Visit our website at www.davidandcharles.co.uk

David & Charles books are available from all good bookshops; alternatively you can contact our Orderline on 0870 9908222 or write to us at FREEPOST EX2 110, D&C Direct, Newton Abbot, TQ12 4ZZ (no stamp required UK only); US customers call 800-289-0963 and Canadian customers call 800-840-5220.

CONTENTS

Introduction

'Cooking,' wrote the great French gastronome Jean Anthelme Brillat-Savarin, 'is an art and adventure.' My own experience has most certainly proved him right. I have also come to agree with the sentiments of the critic John Ruskin that cookery 'means the economy of your grandmothers and the science of the modern chemist; it means much testing and no wasting; it means English thoroughness and French art and Arabian hospitality; and, in fine, it means that you are to be perfectly and always ladies – and loaf givers.'

I learned the basics of cooking and kitchen thrift from my mother, and the art of baking from my aunt Ellen, who was supreme at pastry (especially Yorkshire curd tart) and bread. In the 1960s and early 70s I began experimenting with more ambitious recipes taken from magazines and set myself weekly challenges from the *Cordon Bleu Cookery Course* when it was published as a partwork. I love trying out new ingredients and combinations, but also find I return again and again to the essential principles of cooking that have been passed down by cooks through the ages, and to the old-fashioned comfort foods such as steak and kidney pudding, macaroni cheese and spotted dick, which remain firm favourites with friends and family.

Compared with their forebears, modern cooks have many advantages. Like others of my generation I have vivid childhood memories of putting meat outdoors in winter in the 'meat safe', with its fine mesh front, making cheese by suspending sour milk in a muslin bag and saving up post-war rations of sugar and dried fruit to make a Christmas cake. For the family a regular summer holiday task was skinning homegrown tomatoes for bottling, so that they would keep over the winter. And while I much enjoy making jam and chutney with the fruits and vegetables from our allotment, I am the first to advocate the advantages of the deep freeze, stainless steel knives that stay sharp with little attention and gadgets such as electric food processors and blenders, which cut down massively on the physical effort of tasks such as sieving and beating. Yet no cook, however well equipped their kitchen, can afford to ignore such facts as that a cake will sink if the oven door is opened before the batter is set, that an avocado exposed to the air will turn black, and that just a drop of yolk allowed to mix with egg whites will prevent them from being beaten into a stiff foam.

The 'wise words' I have chosen to include in this book are those that chime with my own experiences. In exploring and expanding on them I have had the pleasure of delving into dozens of cookery and recipe books from the past, including the cookery book published to accompany the gas cooker my mother acquired when she married in 1939. As well as reflecting the culinary tastes of the times, these recipes, such as that for the apple charlotte I still make, reinforce the fact that good cooking never really changes. They have become an inspiration to go back to some of the old dishes.

Time and again I have found myself referring to the great cookery writers and compilers of the past, including Eliza Acton, Mrs Beeton and Fannie Merritt Farmer, the American cook who was the first to explain – and demonstrate through her recipes – the importance of accurate measurement for good results. I have also discovered many other gems, from Alexis Soyer's *Shilling Cookery for the People* to *Kettner's Book of the Table* by the Victorian journalist and critic E. S. Dallas, and *The Modern Cook* by Charles Elmé Francatelli, a pupil of the great French chef Marie-Antoine Carême and *maître d'hotel* and chief cook to Queen Victoria. Also useful have been Mrs A. B. Marshall's *Cookery Book* of 1897; the American cook Maria Parola's 1887 *Kitchen Companion*; *Enquire Within*, the classic late 19th-century Victorian household manual; and *The Constance Spry Cookery Book* by Constance Spry and Rosemary Hume, the first serious cookbook I possessed, which is still well used.

I am, as ever, indebted to my husband Donald, to my daughter Laura and her husband Lewis, and to the many friends who share our table. Thanks are also due to Neil Baber and the team at David & Charles, and to Beverley Jollands for her editorial expertise. This book has given me an unparalleled opportunity to look back to the ways and means of cooks past but also forward to a future in which good home cooking must always have a place.

Ruth Binney
West Stafford, Dorset, 2008

CHAPTER 1

THE PLEASURES OF THE KITCHEN

From stirring a risotto to the smell of toasting spices, and from the sizzle of a steak in the pan to the rhythmic chopping of fresh vegetables, the pleasures of the kitchen take many forms. Above all, the delights of the kitchen are the means of sharing tasty, well-cooked food, created from the best of ingredients, with family and friends. Alexis Soyer, one of the most famous chefs of the mid-19th century, bemoaning the demise of home cooking in a manner reminiscent of today's 'ready meal' culture, concluded that '... a dinner is the creation of a day and the success of a moment. Therefore you will perceive that nothing more disposes the heart to amicable feeling and friendly transactions than a dinner well conceived and artistically prepared.'

To be a good cook it is not necessary to have a kitchen bristling with equipment, although good knives and pans are essential, and such gadgets as electric mixers, food processors and blenders take much drudgery out of food preparation. What is vital, however, is to have a love of food, a knowledge of ingredients and the way they behave and a flair for matching flavours, tastes and textures, so that every dish is a delight to the palate. Compared with the modest range of ingredients available to cooks of previous generations, we are blessed with a vast range of foods from every continent, available in every season of the year. Yet one of the great pleasures of the kitchen is still cooking local foods, and especially those you have grown yourself, and serving them with art and style.

The stove is the cook's most important instrument

Because without it nothing can be cooked. Compared with the stoves and ranges of the past, the heat of modern gas and electric stoves, and even modern ranges, is easy to regulate, making it possible to cook with much greater precision and guarantee consistent results.

The necessity of the stove for cooking was emphasized in books such as *A Plain Cookery for the Working Classes* by Charles Elmé Francatelli, first published in 1852. 'A little sum of money,' he said, should be spent on 'a cooking stove with an oven at the side, or placed under the grate, which should be so planned as to admit of the fire being open or closed at will; by this contrivance much heat and fuel are economized.'

The stove Francatelli describes, with an insulated enclosed grate, is a type of range based on an invention by Count Rumford (born Benjamin Thompson) in 1798, though it would still have been greedy of fuel. Rumford's device, originally used by the German army, consisted of a sheet metal oven set into bricks with small fires underneath each of the hobs on the stovetop and wells sunk into the hotplate to hold pots and pans.

Given the work involved in cleaning out the kitchen range every day, and blacking the outside regularly, the arrival of gas and electric cookers was a boon. Gas cookers, which had been invented in 1802 by

Alexis Soyer, chef of London's Reform Club, invented a small field stove and took it to the Crimea in 1855 to teach the British army how to cook palatable food during the Crimean War. Troops were still using a version of the Soyer Stove at the end of the 20th century.

a Moravian scientist Zachäus Winzler, were slow to catch on, partly because many gas companies, who were supplying gas for lighting, prohibited its use during the day. The stoves became more popular after various models were demonstrated at the Great Exhibition in 1851, and gas cooking became more accurate after the introduction of the thermostat or 'Regulo' in 1923.

The prototype electric cooker, patented in 1879, was the invention of St George Lane-Fox, who discovered how to heat a cooking pot by passing an insulated wire around it. Despite gradual improvements in design, electric cookers did not become popular until the late 1930s.

THE SIZE OF THE KITCHEN HAS NO EFFECT ON THE QUALITY OF THE COOKING

Correct, because a truly good cook can rustle up a wonderful meal on a single ring or even an open fire. But with the luxury of larger kitchens, cooks can treat themselves to an array of good knives, pans and gadgets.

Whatever the size of their kitchen, good cooks are careful to think out in advance what ingredients they need. Instructing beginners, Mary Harrison in *The Skilful Cook*, first published in 1884, says: 'Make, the day before, if possible, a list of articles required for the different dishes, and order what is necessary in good time, so that there may be no delay the next morning. Have the kitchen quite clear from all litters before you begin to work. No one can cook well in a muddle.' She also warns them not to be discouraged by any initial failures. 'Practise,' she writes, 'will give nimbleness to your fingers and strength to your memory. As regards any laughter your mistakes may cause, only persevere, and it will not be long before the laughter is on your side.'

Good cooks make constant use of their taste buds, for there is no other way of making sure that food is well seasoned and full of flavour. A good palate, which has aptly been described as a feather in the cook's cap, can be developed by experimenting with different ingredients and combinations. The ancient Greeks valued the palate so much that they called it *ouranos* – the name they also gave to the heavens.

It is an old saying that the taste of the kitchen is better than its smell.

GADGETS GALORE

Best-loved cooks' gadgets include:

Can opener – invented in the basic 'prise and pierce' form in the 1850s. Types with turning keys and cutting wheels date from 1931.

Electric toaster – arrived in 1893, with bare wires. The pop-up toaster of 1927 had a timer and an electric spring. Thermostatic control came three years later.

Food mixer – invented in 1910 but marketed in its well-designed modern form by Ken Wood in 1950 as the Kenwood Chef.

Food processor – developed in France by Pierre Verdan in the 1960s for the catering industry. In Europe, the Magimix, the domestic version, was launched in 1974. In the USA, Carl Sontheimer's Cuisinart was first sold in 1973.

Electric kettle – said to owe its origin to the British habit of tea drinking. The original model of 1891 had separate chambers for water and the heating element. The Swan kettle of 1922 had the element in a metal tube immersed in the water.

A GOOD COOK ALWAYS WEARS AN APRON

The primary purpose of an apron is to keep clothes free of food stains and smells. If it has pockets an apron is also useful for keeping tools to hand and, in the heat of the moment, can be used as a 'glove' for holding hot pans.

In the days before washing machines, when outer garments were washed infrequently, the apron was essential for keeping clothes clean. Easy to launder, it could be washed by hand every few days. And aprons were not confined to cooks. Even in the early 20th century, schoolteachers, children, shopkeepers and secretaries still wore aprons or pinafores in different styles over their everyday clothing.

In the 1920s and 30s, aprons for women cooks followed the silhouette of the dress beneath, and were long with no waistline. An entry on the subject in *The Concise Household Encyclopedia* of 1933 reflected both the value of the apron and the division of labour within the household: 'Domestic servants require a stock of aprons. Plain white linen is used for nurses, for cooking and general morning wear, and fancy lawn or muslin for parlourmaids, often lace-trimmed or embroidered for afternoon duty.'

By the 1940s fashionable female cooks were wearing aprons with cinched waistlines, often gaily trimmed with rick-rack, buttons, and pockets of contrasting colour.

For cooks who have a garden outside the kitchen door, scooping up the hem of an apron can be handy for bringing in a load of windfall apples, or for taking empty pea and bean pods out to the compost heap or bin.

In the theatre the apron is the part of the stage that projects in front of the curtain, and in architecture the term is used to describe panelling that protects against the weather.

Careful measurements make a perfect cook

A saying that is certainly true when it comes to cakes and baking, and for any other dishes in which the amounts and proportions of ingredients are critical. The experienced cook may want to experiment, but a well-written and properly tested recipe is always a good starting point.

The importance of exact measurements in cooking was recognized in the 19th century. One of the pioneers of accuracy was Fannie Merritt Farmer at her Boston Cooking School for, as she said, 'Correct measurements are absolutely necessary to ensure the best results. Good judgement, with experience, has taught some to measure by sight; but the majority need definite guides.' Miss Farmer recommended 'tin measuring-cups, divided in quarters or thirds, holding one half-pint, and tea and tablespoons of regulation sizes.' She was, furthermore, insistent that cupfuls and spoonfuls of dry ingredients should be measured level, the excess being skimmed off the top with a knife.

Mrs Beeton was also fussy about weighing and measuring, pointing out that, 'Amongst the most essential requirements of the kitchen are scales or weighing-machines for family use.' What was not available to cooks of her era was a means of measuring the temperature of the oven and keeping it constant throughout the cooking period.

The modern cook can weigh out ingredients with electronic scales, which can be adjusted to either imperial or metric measurements. Cooks of the 19th and 20th centuries relied on 'weighing machines' – scales with a bowl on one side and a platform on the other on which weights were put. Similar scales were used in shops to weigh commodities for sale.

The cup measure has remained standard in American recipes and until the 1930s was still widely used in Britain. For cooks without scales or measuring jugs, *Teach Yourself to Cook* of 1948 recommended 'homely measures': a teacup was taken to be ¼ pint and, when filled and levelled, to hold 4oz of a dry ingredient. A piece of butter the size of a hen's egg was estimated to weigh 1¼oz. Since that time, however, British cooks have taken to weighing dry ingredients. Measurement by volume, except for the teaspoon and tablespoon, has disappeared from recipes.

'Weight and measure take away strife.' (Old proverb)

There is a knife for every purpose

For all cooks, knives are the tools of their trade. For versatile cooking, knives are needed in a variety of shapes and sizes, but whatever its purpose a knife should fit comfortably in the hand and have a good balance of weight between handle and blade.

Every cook needs a couple of all-purpose knives, one large and one small. The larger one needs a blade wide enough for jobs such as crushing garlic, and both should have sharp points for making delicate cuts, as when decorating pastry. In all good knives the tang (the part of the blade that extends into the handle) runs the length of the handle and is held in place with rivets. The best modern knives are made of high-carbon stainless steel, which does not rust and is easy to keep sharp. They are expensive but worth the investment.

Knives were traditionally put away during thunderstorms, for fear they would attract lightning.

If you give a knife (or scissors) as a gift it is said that you should demand a penny or other small coin in return: without payment, the gift will sever love.

Before the advent of stainless steel, knives needed to be cleaned carefully to help prevent them from rusting. This was traditionally done on a special knifeboard or rotary cleaner, or with a rag dipped in powdered brick, a substance known as bathbrick.

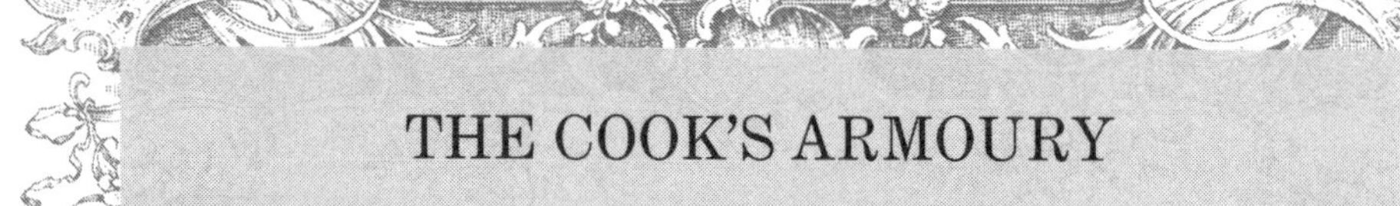

THE COOK'S ARMOURY

Among the other knives a cook will need are:

Filleting knife – a thin, flexible blade at least 18cm (7in) long with a sharp point.

Boning knife – a thin, rigid blade, at least 10cm (4in) long. It needs to be kept razor sharp.

Paring knife – a small knife with a blade about 7.5cm (3in) long. Useful for fruit too soft to prepare with a vegetable peeler.

Cleaver – heavy, with a wide, almost square blade.

Oyster knife – a short, pointed blade with a guard at the base to prevent accidents if the knife slips against a recalcitrant shell.

Palette knife (spatula) – round ended with a flexible blade. The edges should not be sharpened.

Mezzaluna – a wide, curved blade with a short handle at each end, for use with a shallow wooden bowl. Also comes in a two-bladed design.

Carving knife – has a broad, rigid blade at least 20cm (8in) long.

Bread knife – ideally deeply serrated, with a blade 30cm (12in) long. The wide blade comes to a point for 'stabbing' and picking up slices.

Fruit knife – small and serrated, so that it will cut fruit without tearing the flesh, and a pointed blade.

The frying pan is a noisy and greasy servant

For a cook who uses too much oil and allows a pan to get too hot, a frying pan is certainly both noisy and greasy, and extremely dangerous if it catches fire. But when it comes to comfort food, or curing a hangover, there is nothing to beat a good fry-up.

The best frying pans are made of metal and have heavy bases. When shallow frying food (or, more correctly, sautéing it) in a good pan, only a very little oil is needed to stop ingredients sticking and to help crisp and flavour the surface. With deep frying – also called French or wet frying in old cookbooks – immersing food in fat cooks and browns the outside quickly, sealing in the inside and leaving it soft and moist. Cooking food in batter, whether it is homely cod or exotic vegetable tempura, enhances the effect.

Too much noise – and smoke – come from a frying pan that is too hot, which makes an oil thermometer a useful kitchen aid. An ideal temperature for deep frying is 175°C (345°F). Bubbles in a pan of heating fat betray the presence of unwanted water; high quality oil will not bubble and should not smoke. A frying basket is also helpful for making fries and any food covered in egg and breadcrumbs but, as Mary Harrison in *The Skilful Cook* advises, 'fritters, or whatever is dipped in batter, should be dropped into the fat, as they become so light that they rise to the top of it. When they are a pale fawn colour on the one side, they should be turned

To jump out of the frying pan and into the fire, or as the Greeks said 'out of the smoke into the flame' is to go from bad to worse. Each is as hot and burning as the other.

over to the other.' Draining fried food on paper before serving it, to get rid of excess fat, was recommended.

It is a myth that the non-stick frying pan resulted from space technology. Teflon, the first non-stick coating, was discovered by chemists at the US company DuPont in 1938. In 1954 the Frenchman Marc Grégoire began using it to lubricate fishing tackle. It was added to pans from the following year, when Grégoire founded the Tefal company.

THE BEST PANS HAVE HEAVY BASES

True, as long as these don't make them too heavy to lift. The advantage of a heavy base is that the thickness of the metal enables heat to be conducted evenly from pan to food. For long, slow, cooking, a heavy base will retain heat well.

Unlike cheap, thin pans, which dent easily, wear out quickly and burn food by creating 'hot spots', a set of good, heavy pans will not only last a lifetime but produce better food. Of modern materials, stainless steel is the most versatile, and can be used both on top of the stove and in the oven, but for casseroles cast iron with an enamel coating is ideal. Copper gives the best heat conduction of all, but it is expensive and high maintenance since its tin coating needs to be regularly and professionally replaced. Heatproof glass is fine for boiling and baking but does not get hot enough for frying or browning.

A pot boiler was originally a large stone heated in the fire then thrown into a pot to cook food. Now it is a work, usually of pulp fiction, written to make money.

The most ancient pots were probably the heat-resistant shells of terrapins. The first man-made cooking pots were made of clay – among the oldest are those from Japan dating from about 10,000 BC. Food has been cooked in metal pots since at least 100 BC, when the Chinese fashioned their first woks; similar utensils were used in parts of Europe in the same era. By the 1st century AD cooks throughout the Roman Empire were using pans very similar to those of today.

CHOOSE FOODS IN THEIR SEASON

The cook of old, unable to buy Californian strawberries in December or Kenyan beans in February, had no choice but to buy seasonal food. But despite the choice available now, one of the pleasures of cooking is to use flavour-packed local ingredients that fit the mood of the season.

'To be acquainted with the periods when things are in season is one of the most essential pieces of knowledge which enter into the "Art of Cookery".' (Mrs Beeton)

It would be a mistake to think that the shopping list of past times was dull. By the Victorian era many fruits and vegetables were being grown in greenhouses and heated frames, so that forced cucumbers could be purchased in winter, and hothouse apricots, cherries and strawberries in spring and early summer, well before the main crops. Rhubarb was also forced to be ready by February, and some fruits such as oranges and lemons were regularly imported over the winter months, when they were in season in southern Europe.

To ensure that fresh food of some kind was available all year round, crops such as potatoes, onions, marrows, apples and pears were carefully stored. Soft fruit was bottled and made into jam, and meat such as pork was pickled in brine. Fish was smoked and/or dried, while eggs were preserved in isinglass.

DISHES OF THE SEASON

Some 19th-century highlights for seasonal cuisine from Mrs Beeton's suggested 'Bills of Fare':

January – boiled turbot and oyster sauce; haunch of venison; apple tart.

February – fried smelts; roast fowls garnished with watercress; marrow pudding, lemon cream.

March – boiled turbot and lobster sauce; boiled bacon-cheek garnished with spinach; rhubarb tart.

April – croquettes of leveret; larded guinea fowls; orange jelly.

May – boiled mackerel à la Maître d'Hôtel; saddle of mutton; strawberry-jam tartlets.

June – lobster patties; ragout of duck and green peas; strawberry cream.

July – julienne soup; crimped perch and Dutch sauce; stewed veal and peas; raspberry-and-currant tart.

August – fried flounders; stewed shoulder of veal, garnished with forcemeat balls; vol-au-vent of greengages.

September – fillets of turbot à la crème; hare, boned and larded, with mushrooms; compôte of peaches.

October – haddocks and egg sauce; boiled leg of mutton garnished with carrots and turnips; vol-au-vent of pears.

November – eels en Matelote; curried rabbit, apple custard.

December – soles à la crème; boiled turkey and celery sauce; lemon cheesecakes.

Every herb has a perfect partner

A good way of saying that for some ingredients there is a herb that complements its flavour like no other. Even if there is only space for pots on a windowsill, every cook will benefit from growing fresh herbs and having them readily to hand.

It is the specific aromatic notes of herbs – created from a whole spectrum of chemicals, including the essential oils that are released when the leaves are crushed or heated – that help to determine their ideal pairings. Sage, for instance, has a particular affinity with pork fat, cutting and complementing its richness, while the floral scent of rosemary is perfect with lamb. The sharp, citrus notes of fennel and dill give them the ability to highlight fish and shellfish of all kinds, and lemon verbena has even more of a citrus tang. Tarragon and chervil, with their distinctive aniseed taste, are perfect with both eggs and mushrooms, as is the mild onion flavour of chives.

More exotic herbs, now widely available, are essential to oriental cooking, especially fresh coriander (known as cilantro in the USA), which is believed to be the world's most widely used herb and is easy to grow from seed. Its seeds have been found in Bronze Age settlements and even in the tomb of Tutankhamun. Subtle flavour is added with such herbs as lemon grass and kaffir lime leaves and yet more pungent aromas with curry leaves.

Herbs are also essential to some drinks; no Pimms is complete without a sprig of

fresh borage (although mint is a reasonable substitute), while bergamot gives Earl Grey tea its distinctive taste. Mint is key to a mint julep, a cocktail of fresh mint, bourbon, sugar and water. The drink, which originated in the 18th century in the southern USA, was introduced to the wider world at the Round Robin Bar in Washington's Willard Hotel by Senator Henry Clay of Kentucky. It was first described in print in 1803 by an Englishman, John Davis, who wrote *Travels of Four Years and a Half in the United States of America.* He described it as a 'dram of spirituous liquor that has mint in it, taken by Virginians in the morning'. The word 'julep', meaning a sweet drink, comes from the Persian for 'rosewater'.

HERB MIXES

Apart from a classic bouquet garni of parsley, bay leaf and thyme, other herb combinations, sometimes with spices added, are constituents of kitchen classics from different parts of the world:

Fines herbes – France – Tarragon, chervil and chives.

Herbes de Provence – France – thyme, marjoram, fennel, basil, rosemary, lavender.

Pesto – Italy – basil, garlic, pine nuts (without the pine nuts it is a French *pistou*).

Chermoula – Morocco – coriander, onion, garlic, chilli, cumin, saffron, black pepper.

Salsa verde – Italy – parsley, mint, dill and tarragon made into a sauce with capers, breadcrumbs and oil.

Za'atar – Middle East – marjoram, oregano, thyme, sesame, sumac.

A stale spice has little flavour

Which is why it is sensible to buy whole spices in small quantities and to grind or crush them yourself. Whether ready ground or not, all spices are best kept in airtight containers; a well-stocked store cupboard will have all the common spices readily to hand.

Spices, like herbs, are valued in cooking for their distinctive flavours, which come from the aromatic oils contained in different parts of each plant, including roots, bark, fruits, seeds and, in the case of cloves, flower buds. Once a spice is ground these oils evaporate quickly, so diminishing its flavour. For crushing, a small coffee grinder kept specifically for the purpose is ideal, though the traditional implement is a pestle and mortar, a tool mentioned in an Egyptian papyrus of 1550 BC but probably much older than that. For fine grinding, the pestle needs to be heavy with a rough base.

Because of their value (spices were imported from tropical Asia and Africa and were once, ounce for ounce, worth more than gold) ground spices have often been adulterated with inferior 'fillers'. Writing in 1887 the American cook Maria Parloa warns her readers that: 'In this age of adulterations nothing suffers more than ground condiments. The only safety is to buy them at first-class stores. This does not always mean that you will get a pure article, but your chances are much greater than when trusting to the common grocer.'

From the use of spices to flavour confectionery, an old name for sweets is 'spice', as in the nursery rhyme: 'What are little girls made of? Sugar and spice and all things nice.'

Archaeologists have found seeds of spices such as coriander, cumin and fennel in Bronze Age sites, but cannot be sure whether they were used in cooking, for medicine or both. Trade in spices began in Arabia and spread around the world. By the 15th century Venice had become a world power thanks to its control of the Mediterranean spice trade, but lost its domination after the Portuguese and the Dutch discovered new trading routes to the East around the Cape of Good Hope.

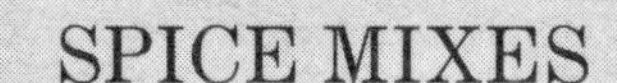

SPICE MIXES

Blends of spices, often with herbs included, give a distinctive character to all kinds of dishes:

Garam masala – the basis for oriental dishes but without heat: cumin, coriander, pepper, black cardamom, cinnamon.

Curry powder – ups the heat with coriander, cumin, cayenne pepper, turmeric and ginger among others.

Fine spices (*épices fines*) – a traditional French mix of white and red pepper, mace, nutmeg, cloves and cinnamon, plus the herbs bay, sage, rosemary and marjoram.

Pickling spice – a mixture for all kinds of preserving, containing allspice, cardamom, cinnamon, cloves, coriander, ginger, mustard seeds and peppercorns. The blend may also contain dried chillis and bay leaves.

SALT SEASONS ALL THINGS

Not just savoury foods, but sweet ones such as cakes and pastries as well. Salt, the cook's essential for flavour, has also been used for millennia as a food preservative.

No kitchen is complete without salt, simple sodium chloride, the white, crystalline chemical that is obtained from seawater and mined from rock deposits worldwide. As well as improving the taste of every savoury dish, a pinch of salt added to the flour in a cake or sweet pastry mixture improves the balance of flavours and, when added to acid fruits such as pineapple and grapefruit, enhances their sweetness.

Adjust the salt in a dish before you serve it, but remember that many people are now deliberately lowering their sodium intake for health reasons. If in doubt, under-salt and leave your guests to add extra at the table.

Sea salt is the kind most prized by connoisseurs, especially when made the traditional way by evaporating seawater in the sun. Table salt is treated with small amounts of magnesium carbonate to keep it flowing freely and may be iodized – that is, have the mineral iodine added as a health benefit.

The history of preserving food by packing it in salt goes back to the Egyptian practice of salting fish, which was being used in the 3rd millennium BC, and in Britain it became the norm during the Iron Age. Salting works by drawing out water, the fluid medium in which microbes flourish, and by killing any that do survive. By the Middle Ages, salt fish was standard fare in Britain and much of Europe; fish were also dried and smoked to become 'red herrings', which would keep undecayed for a twelvemonth.

Don't forget that the perception of saltiness changes with temperature. A perfectly salted hot leek and potato soup will seem tasteless and bland if it is served chilled as a vichyssoise.

DELICIOUSLY SALTY

Many foods from around the world are traditionally preserved with salt:

Salt cod – the *fiel amigo* ('faithful friend') of the Portuguese, who rarely eat fresh cod. It is a traditional boon to Christians banned from eating meat on Fridays and during Lent. In the French dish *brandade de morue*, the fish is poached then pounded with olive oil and milk.

Sauerkraut – shredded cabbage layered with salt and fermented. It is now most strongly associated with German cuisine, but was originally made by the Romans and also by the Chinese.

Bacon – the original was Westphalian ham, produced by Germanic tribes from *Bachen* – wild pigs.

Salami – named from the Italian *salare*, meaning 'to salt'.

Salt beef – once a staple of the British navy, also known as corned beef from the crystals or 'corns' of salt used in its preparation.

Salt pork – one of the basic winter provisions from Roman times onwards; for centuries it was a staple on board ship.

Soy sauce – salt is used in the fermentation of soya beans to make this signature of Asian cooking.

A RISOTTO DEMANDS YOUR UNDIVIDED ATTENTION

One of the great pleasures of cooking is to stand at the stove gently stirring a risotto while it cooks to creamy perfection. As well as devotion, a perfect risotto also needs exactly the right rice. Originally a peasant dish, risotto now features regularly on the menus of the most sophisticated restaurants.

A risotto works because as it cooks starch is removed from the surface of the rice and thickens the liquid in which it is cooked. For this to happen the rice must first be fried in a little oil, so it is sautéed with chopped onion. Hot, well-flavoured stock is then ladled into the rice in small quantities, so that it is gradually absorbed. Meat, fish, shellfish or vegetables are added towards the end of the cooking time. If the risotto is cooked in a large, open pan, plenty of water is boiled off from the stock, intensifying the flavour of the finished dish. When cooked, the rice should still be *al dente* – with a bite. Grated Parmesan is stirred in at the very end and the risotto left to stand for two or three minutes before it is served.

Arborio rice, the favourite of the Italian housewife, is ideal for a risotto because it has big grains with a large surface area that will absorb plenty of liquid. Carnaroli rice is also excellent, and has a firmer texture.

Writing in the early 20th century, Lady Jekyll in her *Kitchen Essays* extolled the versatility of risotto. Of a chicken risotto she says: 'Fragments of pork or of truffles can be brought to the service of this dish, whose infinite variety need never stale with custom.'

Risotto Milanese – saffron risotto – was invented, so the story goes, in 1574, when the city's Gothic cathedral was being built. Valerius, a young apprentice who had been put in charge of staining the glass for the windows, was teased for adding saffron to the glass. Valerius's response was to add saffron to the rice that was to be served at his master's wedding. The result was so good that the technique was quickly adopted by cooks all over the city. The risotto is the traditional accompaniment to *ossobuco* – veal shanks braised in white wine.

Always toss a pancake

Tossing pancakes is part of the ritual of Shrove Tuesday, the day before the beginning of the Lenten fast. Tossing a pancake requires both skill and practice. Eating pancakes, as long as they are followed by 'grey peas' on Ash Wednesday, is said to bring good luck for the year ahead.

Lemon and sugar are the classic pancake accompaniments.

Milk (450ml/1 pint), eggs (3), flour (250g/8oz) and half a teaspoon of salt are the basic ingredients for pancakes, but over the centuries wine, brandy, sugar and cream have all been included for richer results. The batter can be quickly whisked up in a blender, but the old-fashioned method is to put the flour in a bowl, make a well in the centre, add the eggs and milk and beat until the batter is smooth. It then needs to be left to stand for a good half hour to allow the starch grains in the flour to swell and the batter to thicken. In past times, pancakes were cooked in lard, which was prohibited in Lent. A manual of the 1920s perfectly describes the best method of tossing: '. . . shake the pan gently until the pancake slips down over the edge of the pan, give the pan a sharp, upward flick with the wrist, when it will turn completely over into the pan.'

Among the fanciest presentations is the *crêpe Suzette* – a sweet pancake folded and flambéed in an orange sauce containing Grand Marnier. The story that the dish was invented in 1896 for a close female companion of the then Prince of Wales is probably apocryphal. However, the French chef Auguste Escoffier reliably recorded the recipe in 1903.

Russian pancakes, or *blini*, served at their most luxurious with caviar, are made with buckwheat and leavened with yeast. Scots pancakes or drop scones have bicarbonate of soda and cream of tartar added and are often made with buttermilk. Like *blini* they are small enough to need neither tossing nor folding.

A GOOD PASTA DESERVES THE BEST PARMESAN

A grating of fresh Parmesan is indeed the perfect finish to a pasta dish, but only those made with vegetables, meat or other sorts of cheese. Mixing Parmesan with seafood is anathema to purists of Italian cuisine.

The proper name for Parmesan is *grana Parmigiano Reggiano*, which derives from the names of the Parma and Reggio Emilia regions of northern Italy, where the cheese is made. The term *grana* refers to the cheese's grainy texture – the quality that makes it ideal for

In *The Decameron*, his medieval collection of bawdy tales, Giovanni Boccaccio tells of a mountain made entirely of Parmesan. Here the pleasure-obsessed inhabitants of the village of Bengodi spend their entire lives making ravioli and dishes of macaroni boiled in 'capon's broth'.

grating. 'Parmesan' is a French word, which was adopted by the English in the 16th century.

Cheeses of the grana type were developed by medieval monks, who wanted a cheese that would keep well. A tribute to its hardness and good keeping qualities is the fact that that for over 700 years Parmesan has not only been eaten in other parts of Italy but also exported much farther afield. Its production is strictly controlled: only about 500 artisan cheesemakers around the Po Valley have the right to call their cheese Parmigiano Reggiano, and the milk of the cows that graze in the designated area is too valuable to drink: it is all turned into cheese, and milk for all other purposes is imported.

Good Parmesan has a flavour that is sharp and fruity, not bitter like the cheese that comes ready grated in cartons. Ideally it should be bought in small quantities and when *con gocciola* – that is, when tiny drops of moisture can be seen on the surface when the cheese is split open. Parmesan makes an authentic addition to a minestrone, and thrifty Italian cooks save the rinds to add to the pan while the soup is cooking. Soft Parmesan can be sliced in thin curls and used to finish a salad, but there are few dishes more satisfying than a simple dish of tagliatelle with butter, sage, cream and Parmesan. The perfect host or hostess will add Parmesan to guests' pasta at the table, using a grater designed specifically for the purpose.

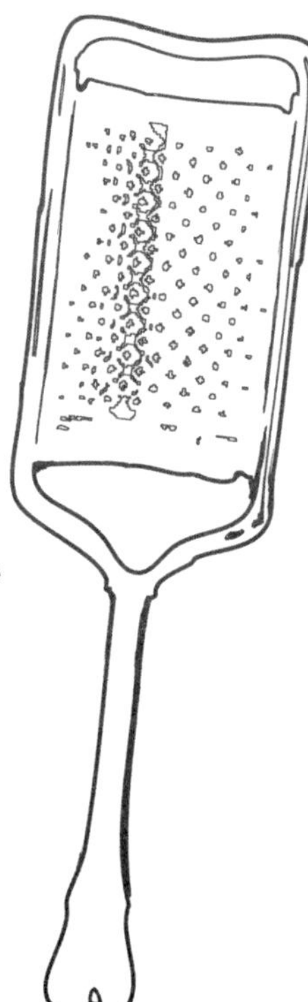

In 1666, Samuel Pepys hastily buried his precious Parmesan in the garden before making his escape during the Great Fire of London, and in the last years of his life the French playwright Molière (who died in 1673) would eat nothing else.

A clear soup can never be too transparent

The rule for a perfect consommé, a term invented by the French in the 16th century from *consommer*, meaning 'to finish'. It is indeed the clearing or finishing that not only converts an ordinary stock into a consommé but also ensures both the transparency of the dish and the excellence of the cook's ability.

A classic consommé begins with a broth initially made with meat and meat bones (or fish and fish bones), and with vegetables added for the last hour of a four-hour cooking time. The pan is skimmed of any scum that forms, the liquid cooled and any fat removed. Then, as Fannie Merritt Farmer instructs: '. . . put quantity to be cleared in stew-pan, allowing white and shell of one egg to each quart of stock. Beat egg slightly, break shell in small pieces and add to stock.' After bringing the mixture to a hard boil for two minutes, and simmering and skimming for another 20, she recommends that you should 'strain through double thickness of cheese cloth placed over a fine strainer' and that 'many think the flavor obtained from a few shavings of lemon rind an agreeable addition'.

Consommé chemistry: the egg white and shell work because the albumen they contain traps the proteins that cloud the original stock, forming a kind of mesh that can then be strained off. Adding more meat instead of eggs – as the Chinese do – works in a similar way.

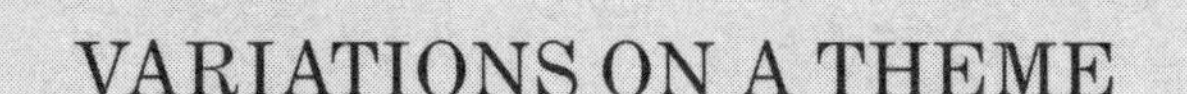

VARIATIONS ON A THEME

When the consommé is clear, further ingredients can be added, as you please. Among the many consommés in Fannie Farmer's repertoire were:

Consommé Royale – soup served with a 'Royal Custard', which was made with egg yolks and a little of the prepared consommé, flavoured with a grating of nutmeg and a hint of cayenne.

Consommé au Parmesan – finished with small Parmesan-flavoured choux paste 'dumplings' made from milk, lard, butter, flour and egg and deep fried by the teaspoonful.

Consommé aux Pâtes – served with noodles, macaroni or other pasta, which was cooked separately before being added. (With julienne vegetables this becomes a minestrone.)

Consommé Colbert – with the addition of cooked green peas, flageolet beans and cubes of carrots and celery, and with a poached egg served in each dish of soup.

Consommé Princess – with green peas and diced chicken included.

Consommé with Vegetables – served with French string beans, and cooked carrots cut into fancy shapes using French vegetable cutters.

A WOMAN WHO HAS MASTERED SAUCES SITS ON THE APEX OF CIVILIZATION

And a man too, for whatever the sex of the chef it is their ability to make sauces that transforms dishes from the mundane to the magnificent. The simplest sauces consist of puréed fruit, as in an apple sauce, or a sieved or puréed mixture of cooked vegetables, as in a tomato sauce. But for sophistication of flavour and texture there is much more to a sauce than this.

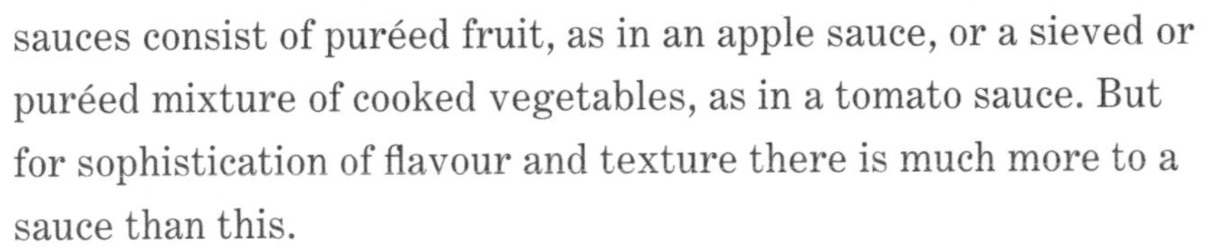

Classic French cookery divides hot, thickened savoury sauces into two categories: white and brown, or *velouté* and *Espagnole*. The basis of the white (or French butter) sauce is a roux, made with butter and flour, to which is added hot milk – either alone or mixed with a quantity of meat, fish or vegetable stock, or wine, until the required consistency is reached. The adept cook will stir the sauce constantly to avoid lumps. The sauce can then be flavoured as desired, with spices, herbs, lemon juice or anything from cheese to capers and cucumber. Alternatively, a plain velouté may be added to any savoury mixture of your choice.

The term Espagnole *is said by some to date from the reign of Louis XV, when Spanish ham bones were the favoured ingredient for making the stock.*

A basic brown sauce is made in a similar way to a white one, but the roux is cooked for longer, until it is a light coffee colour. Hot, concentrated, well-reduced stock, ideally made using browned meat bones as its basis, is then added. The sauce can be finished with wine, port or other alcohol as you desire, and all kinds of vegetables and meat can be added.

The other way of thickening a sauce is with egg yolks and butter, as with a béarnaise. For this, vinegar and white wine are put in a pan with chopped shallots and tarragon then cooled. Egg yolks are added and the pan put over hot water (a *bain marie*). Butter is then added a little at a time until the sauce thickens, but it must not boil or the egg will scramble.

SAUCY SAYINGS

Almost every cookery writer has something pertinent to say about the making of sauces:

'The preparation and appearance of sauces and gravies are of the highest consequence.' (Mrs Beeton)

'A sauce should have so pleasant a flavour and be so discreetly blended that on tasting you feel it might be eaten by itself.' (Constance Spry and Rosemary Hume)

'Gravy, or the juice of meat, is always a sauce, although a sauce is not always a gravy.' (George Augustus Sala)

'Melted butter (French butter sauce) can be multiplied *ad infinitum*, according to the ability of the artist.' (Alexis Soyer)

'Garlic, when very sparingly and judiciously used, imparts a remarkably fine savour to a sauce or gravy.' (Eliza Acton)

'The true epicurean way of eating fresh salmon and trout [is to] use only a little vinegar and mustard.' (Salmonia Davy)

Summer is not complete without strawberries and cream

Certainly so in England, where the combination is synonymous with tennis at Wimbledon. In America strawberries are added to whipped cream as a filling for a classic strawberry shortcake.

The tradition of eating strawberries and cream at Wimbledon, home of the All England Tennis Club, goes back to the inception of the tournament in 1877, when it was little more than a garden party with some tennis on the side. Today, approximately 2,800kg (62,000lb) of strawberries and 24,650 litres (1,540 gallons) of cream are sold and consumed during the two weeks of the championships each year.

It is said that strawberry shortcake was 'invented' long ago by American Indians, who mashed the berries into flour, making a kind of bread. These must have been wild strawberries, since the cultivated fruits we know today date only from the 17th century. Wild ones (such as *Fragaria vesca* – *fraga* means 'fragrant') grow in both the Old and New Worlds, and although breeding began in the 14th century the breakthrough came with the discovery of the plump Virginia strawberry (*F. virginiana*), which was crossed with the even juicier south American pine or beach strawberry (*F. chiloensis*).

The recipe for today's strawberry shortcake dates back to the 1850s. It is reliably recorded in the *Ladies' New Receipt Book* by Eliza Leslie, an American cook fond of introducing French ideas. For the dish she used a mixture that was a

Before toothpaste, strawberry juice was used to help remove tartar from the teeth and to fade freckles and other marks on the skin. Herbalists of old used the fruit to treat everything from melancholy to fevers.

cross between a pastry and a biscuit (cookie) dough, slightly sweetened. This was rolled out thickly and cut into rounds. When cooked, each was split into two thin layers, which were sandwiched with mashed, sweetened strawberries. In these early versions, cream would have been served on the side.

Make Christmas puddings on Stir-up Sunday

The date in question is the last Sunday in the Christian calendar, the Sunday before Advent, when the prayers for the day include the one that begins: 'Stir up we beseech thee, O Lord, the wills of thy faithful people . . .'

Everyone in the household, it is said – including babies, with a helping hand – should stir the Christmas pudding mixture for luck before it is cooked. Three stirs, made deeply enough to reveal the bottom of the basin, and a silent wish are still the requirements in some families.

A Christmas pudding needs long, slow cooking so that all the suet in the mixture melts before the particles in the flour burst open. After cooking it should be doused with brandy to help it keep and mature well.

Today's Christmas pudding is a rich version of the plum puddings first made in the 15th century, which became associated with the festive season from about 1670. Suet is the only reminder that the original puddings (like mince pies) included meat. A typical early mixture would have been chopped mutton or beef, onions, dried fruit and breadcrumbs, possibly with root vegetables added.

Flaming the Christmas pudding with brandy harks back to the origin of Christmas as a pagan festival of light. Because of this association the Puritan ruler Oliver Cromwell banned the eating of puddings on Christmas Day in the 1650s. He also forbade the use of meat in mincemeat as an unacceptable indulgence.

The traditional round shape of Christmas puddings comes from the way they were originally cooked – they were tied up in a pudding cloth and boiled.

SERVE HOT FOOD ON HOT PLATES

Because otherwise the food will quickly go cold and become unappetizing, although the good host or hostess will ensure that plates are not so scaldingly hot that guests risk injury.

In the days when cooking was done on a range (as it is today with an Aga), it was easy to put plates in the coolest oven to warm while food was being cooked. The invention of the 'hostess trolley' in the 1950s was a boon for entertaining as it could keep both food and plates warm, allowing the hostess time to entertain her guests before the meal was served. By the mid-1970s these trolleys had become so popular that they were the favourite Christmas gifts for housewives.

Ensuring that food is hot when it reaches the table adds to the pleasure of eating because it allows the aromas to reach your nose and stimulate your appetite before you even taste the first mouthful. As the French gastronome Jean Anthelme Brillat-Savarin observed, 'Without the cooperation of smell there can be no complete degustation.'

The 'good student of cooking' was given copious instructions on dishing food in classic cookbooks such as the *Constance Spry Cookery Book*, published in 1956. 'Do not in anxiety to feel unhurried,' it says, 'start dishing too early so that you are faced with the tiresome problem of keeping things hot . . . Rather have everything quite ready, then dish neatly and quickly and serve right away.'

A DINNER TABLE SHOULD BE WELL LAID AND WELL LIT

. . . to ensure that your guests enjoy their food, and the company at table, to the maximum. Giving attention to the table before dinner guests arrive, and including all the 'extras' such as pepper and salt, will also relieve hosts of last-minute panics while they are putting the finishing touches to their dishes.

Until the 16th century, knives (and fingers) were the only cutlery used at table. Forks were introduced to British tables in the early 17th century, probably by the traveller and author Thomas Coryat.

The simple rule, when setting the table, is to lay out the knives, forks and spoons in the order in which they will be used, from the outside in. The spoon and fork for dessert may go at the top of each place setting (also known as a 'cover'), with the spoon uppermost, handle to the right. Glasses are set out for each guest, for white and red wine and for water. This arrangement, known as *service à la russe*, with each course of the meal brought to the table sequentially, first appeared in England and France in the mid-19th century and by the late 1890s was regularly followed. Before this, the norm had been *service à la française*, which dated from the Middle Ages, in which a large number of dishes were put on the table at once, from which diners helped themselves.

When laying a table, care about detail pays off. For, as it states in *Enquire Within*: 'The whiteness of the table-cloth, the clearness of glass, the polish of plate and the judicious distribution of ornamental groups of fruits and flowers, are matters deserving the utmost attention.'

Ornate napkin folding may be the vogue, but there is no need to concern yourself with it. Providing good quality linen or damask is much more important. As Emily Post said in *Etiquette* (1922): 'Very fancy foldings are not in good taste.' As to placement, she advised that the napkin should be arranged on each service plate: 'Napkins are put at the side,' she said, 'only when it is necessary to put food on the table before seating the guests . . . Bread should not be put on the napkin.' As for lighting, it needs to be subtle enough to add to the atmosphere but not so dim as to make it impossible to see and converse with other guests. Candles give a nice light, but need to be safe.

CHAPTER 2

TASTY MEAT AND FISH

Whether roasted or grilled, braised or stewed, meat and fish are the focus of most main courses and important sources of protein in the diet. Because they are the most expensive items on most shopping lists, quality is also vital. Meat must be wholesome and well hung, so that it is tender and tasty when cooked, and fish and shellfish spanking fresh. Prudent cooks will make friends with their local butcher and fishmonger, and shop at farmers' markets to ensure that their ingredients are as good as possible and prepared just as they want them – beef ribs chined, fish filleted and so on.

As for the cooking, instructions and wise words to the cook abound. One sensible rule, which is fine for all but grilled and pan-fried meats such as steaks, is 'Cook fish quickly, meat slowly.' Such treatment should ensure that the tissues of meat break down and that its fat melts, and that fish remains firm and moist. Miss Maria Parloa, one of the most popular cookery teachers and cookbook authors of 19th-century America, maintained that, 'Were it possible to teach every housekeeper how to boil, roast and broil meat properly, one might be satisfied that a life's work had been accomplished. In ninety out of a hundred households,' she complains, 'grades of meat, from the choicest to the coarsest pieces, are ruined every day of the week.' For fish, her rule was that the lighter the fish the more simply it should be cooked, it being 'almost shameful to attempt to improve anything so delicate and fine in itself'.

A MARINADE WILL TENDERIZE ANY MEAT

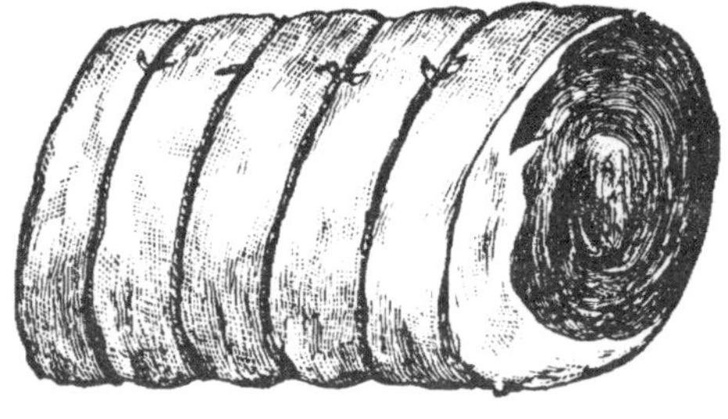

And if oily it will improve the taste and texture of very lean meat such as venison or skinless chicken breast. If it contains acid ingredients such as lime juice, a marinade will 'cook' raw fish, to create a dish known as a ceviche.

In medieval times, fish was commonly marinated after it was cooked. The modern equivalents are soused herrings and escabeche, a dish particularly loved in Spain, for which the marinade is generally a mixture of sweet and sour, often with nuts and raisins added.

A marinade is a well-seasoned liquid in which meat, game or fish is immersed before it is cooked. The most usual ingredients for a marinade are wine, lemon or lime juice, oil, fresh or dried herbs, spices and chopped vegetables such as onions, garlic and celery. It is the acid ingredients that tenderize flesh by breaking down muscle fibres and softening the tissues between them, while the oil keeps the flesh moist. In the days before refrigerators, the salt in a marinade would also work as a useful preservative.

Marinades may be cooked or uncooked. A typical cooked marinade, in which red meat can be marinated for up to 48 hours, might consist of red wine, olive oil, sliced shallot, crushed peppercorns, juniper berries and salt, boiled together and cooled before use.

A cold marinade for a ceviche might be a mixture of lime juice, white wine vinegar, crushed garlic, chopped coriander (cilantro), salt and freshly ground pepper. Because the acid in these mixtures can react with some metals, it's advisable to use a glass, ceramic or enamelled container when marinading meat or fish.

Test roast beef with your fingers

Pressing a joint of beef in this way will give you a good idea of how pink it will be in the middle. Rare meat will still have plenty of 'give', but if it is well done it will be harder. For really accurate testing, a meat thermometer is an invaluable tool.

Before cooking a joint of beef you need to weigh the meat to calculate the time it will need, and preheat the oven to 190°C/375°F/Gas 5. For rare allow 11 minutes per 450g (1lb), plus 10 minutes, for medium allow 14 minutes per 450g (1lb) plus 10 minutes and for well done 16 minutes per 450g (1lb) plus 10 minutes. If you are using a meat thermometer, insert it into the thickest part of the meat. Temperatures to aim for are: rare 60°C (140°F); medium 70°C (160°F); well done 80°C (175°F).

Yeomen of the Guard, appointed bodyguards for the coronation of Henry VII in 1485 and as Warders of the Tower of London by Edward VI, are popularly known as Beefeaters. On duty at the Tower, they still wear uniforms dating from Tudor times.

The 'roast beef of Old England' is legendary, and the English reputation for the dish (though not for the country's cuisine in general) is recorded in comments such as this one from Per Kalm, a visitor from Sweden in 1748: 'The English men understand almost better than any other people the art of properly roasting a joint, which is also not to be wondered at; because the art of cooking as practised by most Englishmen does not extend much beyond roast beef and plum pudding.'

Yorkshire pudding is the traditional accompaniment to roast beef and was once cooked under the meat – that is, put in the oven on a separate shelf below the joint. When times were hard this batter pudding would be served to the family with gravy before the beef was carved, so as to fill empty stomachs and make the meat stretch further.

The shorter the fibres, the more tender the flesh

A handy rule for judging the quality of the butcher's meat, but not the only important factor. The cut is critical, as is, for beef especially, the length of time the meat has been hung.

Meat is muscle, made of bundles of long, thin fibres, which are supported by sheets of connective tissue containing collagen. Age and exercise toughen muscle fibres – by increasing the number of fibres in every muscle bundle – but with age comes the deposition of fat, the 'marbling' that melts in cooking and adds to meat's succulence. Animal anatomy is also significant. The muscles of the forequarters, which the animal uses more, are generally tougher and more packed with collagen than those of the rump or those near the spine and under the backbone.

Cuts such as steaks combine the advantages of being from the rump of the animal and having short fibres. Slicing meat across the grain, as in a T-bone steak or meat sliced for a stroganoff or a Chinese stir-fry, helps to create short fibres which, though probably already tender, are extremely easy to chew. Tenderness also depends on an animal's health. A well-fed creature will have plump muscle fibres packed with the carbohydrate glycogen. In the carcass this is converted into lactic acid, which tenderizes the flesh by breaking down the protein in the muscle fibres, and helps prevent it being infected with bacteria.

With hanging, enzymes are released that add both acidity and tenderness to the meat. You can judge well-hung beef by its deep, not bright, red colour. Beef can safely be hung for up to six or even eight weeks, but today's commercial pressures make three weeks the norm.

In the 1940s two young entrepreneurs paid a small sum to a Californian restaurateur for his 'magic formula' – a substance for tenderizing cheap cuts of meat. So began the widescale sale of meat tenderizers based on the papaya enzyme, though for centuries before this the people of South and Central America had been improving their meat by wrapping it in papaya leaves.

Every roast needs a good gravy

The simplest and best sauce to serve with any roast when made from the juices of the meat. If left unthickened it is known as 'God's gravy'. The juices of beef have been dubbed 'Nelson's blood' and given to children, direct from the serving spoon, to build up their strength.

Our grandmothers made their gravy by adding flour to the fatty residue in the roasting pan to make a roux, then adding any meat juices and well-seasoned stock to make a sauce. For an unthickened gravy or *jus* the pan is simply deglazed with stock. Before the 16th century a common practice was to boil meat to create a stock, then roast it. A century later, cooks were roasting meat from scratch but cutting into it when partly cooked to collect the juices. By the 18th century stock was being made from bones and scraps of meat.

The raggedly clothed Bisto Kids of the famous advertising campaign were created by cartoonist Wilf Owen in 1919. Catching the whiff of gravy in the air, they exclaim 'Ah Bisto!'

The importance of making stock for gravy was acknowledged by Eliza Acton in her recipe for 'Gravy in Haste', which reads: 'Chop fine a few bits of lean meat, a small onion, a few slices of carrot and turnip, and a little thyme and parsley; put these with half an ounce of butter into a thick saucepan, and keep them stirred until they are slightly browned; add a little spice, and water in the proportion of a pint to a pound of meat; clear the gravy from scum, let it boil half an hour, then strain it for use.' To assist gravy making, caramelized gravy brownings were manufactured. In 1908 came Bisto, the meat-flavoured gravy powder whose name is an acronym – it 'Browns, Seasons and Thickens in One'.

GREAT GRAVIES

Gravy can be served in a jug or, more traditionally, with a ladle from a gravy boat. All these are tasty variations:

Onion gravy – lightly browned softened onions in a gravy made with stock and wine. Best with sausages or steak or other red meat.

Giblet gravy – made with stock from the giblets of poultry, especially turkey.

Redeye gravy – the pan drippings of fried ham deglazed with coffee. A gravy of the southern USA.

White gravy (also called cream, country or sawmill gravy) – meat drippings thickened with white flour, and usually with milk or cream added. An American accompaniment to biscuits (scones), also served with chicken, fried ham or steak.

Cold gravy – a gravy made from calves' feet, which sets when cold – essentially aspic.

You can't overcook pork

In other words, make sure that the meat is really well cooked through. Historically, the reason was that 'measly' pig meat harboured the eggs of tapeworms, which, if not killed by heat, could hatch out in the human intestine with disastrous consequences.

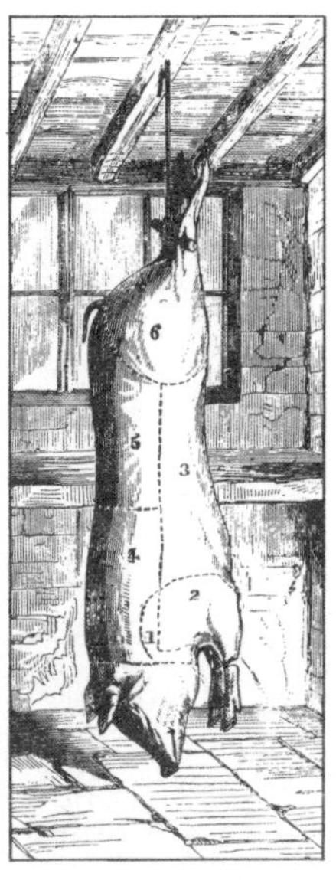

We can be sure, today, that the pork we buy from the supermarket is safe to eat, but it has not always been so, especially in hot weather. In his *Shilling Cookery for the People* of 1854 Alexis Soyer recommended watching out for 'little kernels' in the fat – the tell-tale signs of measliness – and warned against 'clammy and moist' flesh. Rather than touching the meat he suggested poking it with a wooden skewer, then allowing the nose to test for freshness.

To serve with pork, whether a roast or chops, apple sauce and sage and onion stuffing, both of which cut through the fattiness of the meat, are long-favoured accompaniments that are without equal. In Germany and other European countries, caraway is a popular seasoning, and cabbage of some kind, including sauerkraut, is a traditional accompaniment. The Italians and Spanish still cook their pork in milk.

The pig has long held the reputation of being a lazy, gluttonous and unclean animal. Moses, as recorded in the Book of Leviticus, expressly forbade the Israelites from eating pork, declaring that, 'although it is a hoofed animal with cloven hoofs' the pig is unclean because 'it does not chew the cud'. Pigs, being versatile, unfussy feeders and easy to keep, were bred for food by the ancient Chinese in the 3rd century BC. Even in the mid-19th century pigs roamed freely around New York's Upper East Side, foraging for edible scraps.

> It is said that there is a use for every part of a pig – except the squeak.

Cool a ham in its cooking liquid

A good way of ensuring that the meat of a boiled ham that is to be served cold stays moist and succulent. The secret of all good ham, whether cooked or, like Parma ham, eaten raw, lies in the way in which the fresh meat is prepared. Making ham was another of the old country ways of keeping pork over the winter.

The ham or amateur actor is probably named from a derisory term – a 'hamfatter' – mentioned in an old minstrel song called 'The Ham Fat Man'. Ham fat was used to remove stage makeup.

Salting and drying the hind leg of a pig is a technique that has been practised since the days of ancient Rome, if not earlier. In the 2nd century BC the statesman Cato advised: 'Spread salt on the bottom of the jar or pot; then lay a ham, with the skin facing downwards, and cover the whole with salt. Place another ham over it and cover in the same way, taking care that meat does not touch meat. Continue in the same way until all are covered. When you have arranged them all, spread salt above so that the meat shall not show, and level the whole.' After salting they were to hang 'for two days in a draught. On the third day,' he said, 'clean them thoroughly with a sponge and rub with oil. Hang them in smoke for two days, and the third day take them down, rub with a mixture of oil and vinegar, and hang in the meat-house. No moths or worms will touch them.'

Some types of ham are smoked over wood as part of the drying process. For this, woods such as hickory and oak are favoured, and in Ireland peat is used, which imparts an earthy taste. Ham for cooking is not nearly as salty today as in times past, when it had to be soaked in water overnight to get rid of the excess salt. Ham was often cooked in cider to give a good flavour. One modern version of this, pioneered by Nigella Lawson, is to cook it in Coca Cola.

A MATTER OF PLACE

Some of the world's best and most famous hams can be traced to a specific location, even if these now simply describe a style of curing:

Cooked hams

Bradenham ham – an English ham cured with molasses and juniper berries. It has been made since 1781, to a recipe invented by Lord Bradenham, at Chippenham in Wiltshire.

Jambon de Paris – a wet-cured, lightly smoked French ham.

Smithfield ham – a type of Virginia ham named for a small town on the James River, dry-salted and smoked with hickory and apple wood.

York ham – a dry-salted, smoked style of English ham now cured in many parts of the world.

Raw hams

Parma ham (*proscuitto di Parma*) – cured with sea salt then dried, but not smoked. Authentic Parma ham is stamped with the *consorzio* mark.

Serrano ham (*jamón serrano*) – Spanish ham whose name literally means 'mountain ham'. Made from the meat of white pigs.

Bayonne ham (*jambon de Bayonne*) – an air-dried, salted, lightly smoked ham named for the ancient city port of Bayonne in the Basque country.

Westphalian ham (*Westfälische Schinken*) – a dark-coloured German ham, dry salted, then brined and smoked over beech and juniper wood.

MARRY ROAST LAMB WITH MINT SAUCE

One of the best combinations, not only for flavour but to make the meat, which except for the leg is quite fatty, more digestible. The health benefits of mint have long been appreciated for curing such ailments as colic, dyspepsia, headaches, hiccups and heartburn.

In mythology, the nymph Minta was loved by the god Hades, but his jealous wife Persephone turned her into a plant that would always live in the shade.

The practice of serving herbs with lamb and mutton is an old one, and mint is an essential ingredient of Middle Eastern lamb dishes. Its use was spread across Europe by the Romans, and in Elizabethan times it was strewn around the floors to sweeten the air. In the 17th century it was one of the 'precious herbs' taken, for its medicinal properties, from England to Massachusetts.

Although the herbalist John Gerard wrote in 1633 that 'the smell of mint does stir up the mind and the taste to a greedy desire of meat', the practice of serving mint sauce with lamb dates only from the 19th century. In Gerard's era the French chef and author François Pierre de la Varenne recommended finishing the cooking of a daube of leg of mutton with *fines herbes* and lemon or orange rind.

Mint sauce is no more than a mixture of mint, sugar and vinegar, but if you have a garden you can grow mints of different flavours, such as apple, basil and eau de cologne, to add subtlety to your sauce.

In both Christianity and Islam, lamb is a festival food. As a metaphor for Christ, the Pascal lamb, it is the traditional food for the Christian Easter festival. On Eid-el-Adha, the Islamic festival commemorating the sacrifice of Abraham, a sheep is roasted and shared among the community, including the poor.

Flatten escalopes with a rolling pin

A handy way of beating any kind of meat thinly if you don't possess a meat mallet – a wooden bat fashioned explicitly for such tasks.

The ideal thickness for an escalope, because it needs to cook quickly, is about 5mm (¼in). Even more important is that it should be cut across the grain. Beating the meat between sheets of cling film or greaseproof paper helps prevent it from damage.

Of all the dishes based on escalopes, among the most famous is the Italian *saltimbocca*, in which pieces of veal are each covered with a sage leaf and rolled in prosciutto so tasty that they 'jump into the mouth', hence the name of the dish. A similar but more complex English 19th-century version of the dish was veal olives. A typical recipe for thin slices of veal fillet from Richard Dolby's *Cook's Dictionary* of 1833 reads: '. . . rub them over with yolks of egg, strew on them some breadcrumbs, mixed with parsley chopped, lemon peel grated, pepper, salt, and nutmeg; on every piece lay a thin slice of bacon, it must not be too fat; roll them up tight, fasten them with small skewers, rub the outside with egg and roll them in breadcrumbs.' He recommended cooking them in the oven or frying them and serving them with a good gravy.

The term 'escalope' was originally coined to describe thin pieces of veal but is now also used for pork, chicken and turkey.

The German name for the escalope is *Schnitzel*, best known as the *Wienerschnitzel*, or Viennese cutlet, in which the meat is coated in egg and breadcrumbs and fried. In fact this famous dish may have originated in Milan as the *cotoletta alla Milanese* before being introduced to Austria in the 15th or 16th century. An alternative theory is that it was introduced in 1857 by the Austrian Field Marshal Josef Radetzky, who commanded the Imperial Austrian garrison in Milan.

Veal, the flesh of calves, has been eaten since Roman times. It has a delicate flavour and texture and is low in fat. It has declined greatly in popularity in many countries due to concerns over rearing methods, where calves are kept confined in crates and pumped with hormones and antibiotics.

ADD DUMPLINGS FOR A FINE STEW

Dumplings are indeed a great addition to a stew and a way of making it even more rib-sticking and satisfying. They can also be cooked in a stock or soup, or even in boiling water.

The basic dumpling is a ball of dough. Originally this was probably bread dough raised with yeast, but it could be made with nothing more than flour and water (for a Suffolk or hard dumpling). It could also contain suet, potato, semolina or oatmeal. In central Europe dumplings are an old way of using up stale bread, which is soaked in water or milk then mixed with egg and, possibly, chopped meat, liver or cheese. From the earliest times, herbs have been added to dumplings, and sometimes chopped wild greens such as young dandelions and nettles.

'A dinner should begin with broth and white suet dumplings boiled in the broth with the beef, then the meat itself . . . the beef came last of all, only to those who had done justice to the broth and the ball.' (Mrs Gaskell, Cranford)

In English cookery dumplings are invariably served with boiled beef and as such are the equivalent of the Yorkshire pudding served with a joint of roast beef. Norfolk dumplings are a richer variety, made with eggs, flour and milk to form a batter, which is dropped by the spoonful into boiling water. Accompaniments suggested by Eliza Acton included wine sauce and melted butter with vinegar added.

'Yeast dumplings must not boil too fast, as they then might boil out of the pot.' (Charles Elmé Francatelli)

Asian dumplings are quite different from the western variety, being filled parcels more like ravioli. Chinese wontons, one of the most popular kinds, are made from sheets of wheat dough filled, typically, with minced pork and onions. The habit of leaving the edges wavy gives them their name, which is a pun on the word for chaos.

STEW BOILED IS STEW SPOILED

Long and low is the cook's guide for guaranteeing tender meat in stews and casseroles. If the pot is allowed to boil hard the meat becomes stringy, because the muscle fibres of which meat is composed shrink quickly, making them tough.

The stew has long been favoured by both busy and cost-conscious cooks. It can be left to simmer untended on a low heat, and can make even the most unpromising ingredients palatable. As the meat cooks, the tough collagen – the tissue that holds the bundles of muscle fibres together – is broken down into succulent gelatine. At the same time, the fat in the meat melts, deliciously infusing any potatoes or root vegetables added to the pot with its flavour.

Stews have their origins in the tradition of cooking over an open fire, their ingredients depending on local agriculture and climate. In the Irish stew, neck of mutton or kid are therefore the key ingredients,

The casserole is named for the pot in which it is cooked, originally a French copper cooking pot, often ostentatiously displayed on the wall to advertise the wealth of its owner rather than being used on the stove.

plus potatoes, onions and a little water. No carrots, barley, leeks or other ingredients should, purists argue, be added, and when the stew is cooked all the water should be absorbed by the potatoes, converting them into a thick, creamy mash.

For a fish stew, such as the delicious Mediterranean bouillabaisse, gentle heat is needed not for tenderizing the ingredients but to make sure that the fish does not disintegrate into the cooking liquid.

Any kidney is best devilled

That is, flavoured with spices. Devilled kidneys, served on toast, became a popular hearty breakfast dish in Victorian times. Beef kidneys are a component of the essential filling for substantial meat pies and suet puddings.

Lamb's kidneys, which have a milder flavour than those of the pig or ox, are ideal for devilling. For an authentic result they need to be fried in butter with a mixture of Worcestershire sauce, mushroom ketchup, cayenne pepper, English mustard powder, salt and black pepper. A less spicy mixture, served on toast, was popular as a savoury, when this course was routinely served at the end of a dinner. A typical recipe called for minced veal kidneys with fried minced onion pounded with salt, pepper and chopped parsley, mixed with beaten egg and heated through until cooked.

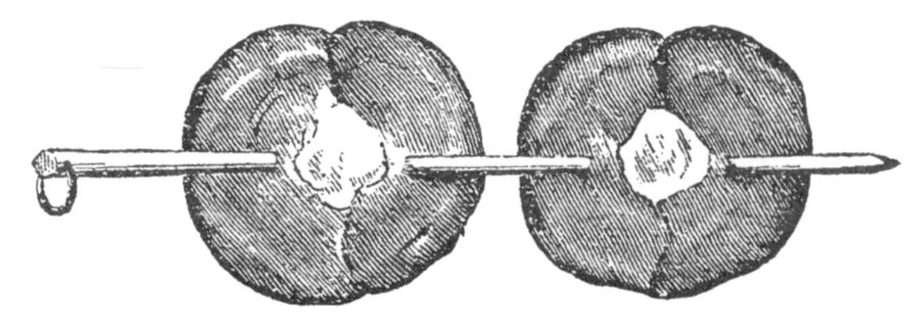

For a steak and kidney pie or pudding, chopped ox kidney is the best choice. Puff pastry is the cook's preferred selection for a pie; for a steamed pudding it is suet crust, made with a mixture of chopped beef suet (the fat from around the kidneys) and cold water, allowing 150–175g (5–6oz) suet for every 450g (1lb) flour. The pudding needs to be steamed for at least four hours, and is, says Mrs Beeton, 'very much enriched by adding a few oysters or mushrooms'. For the poor, a pudding made with kidneys alone was an economical treat.

To improve the flavour of ox kidneys it helps to soak them in cold water for several hours, or even overnight. The consensus on cooking all kidneys is that for a tender result they should either be cooked very quickly or very slowly.

Prick sausage skins to stop them bursting

A useful precaution if sausages are not of the highest quality, and for any sausages to be cooked at high temperatures, but pricking allows the juices to leak from good sausages, reducing their succulence.

The more water there is in a sausage the more likely it is to burst when it is cooked. Sausages earned their nickname of 'bangers' when, during the 1940s, they were so packed with water that they were likely to explode when heated. Modern sausage makers recommend no pricking and slow frying or cooking under a moderate grill to prevent the skins from bursting.

An old method of toughening sausage skins or casings – made from animal intestines or, as Fanny Farmer called them, 'prepared entrails' – was to dip them in boiling water before they were cooked. Alternatively, they were pricked first, then boiled until done.

Many culinary regions have characteristic types of sausage which relate closely to the climate. So it is no accident that dried sausages that keep well, such as salami, originated in warm countries such as Italy and Spain. The Frankfurter is named for Frankfurt am Main, but 'hot dog' entered the vocabulary when, in 1906, the American cartoonist Tad Dorgan depicted a sausage dog (a dachshund) served up in a bun.

The expression 'not a sausage', which when first coined meant lack of money, relates back to cockney rhyming slang, in which bangers and mash equal cash.

A quintessentially English sausage dish is toad-in-the-hole, which is made from sausages baked in batter. Described by Mrs Beeton as 'homely but savoury' (she used steak and kidney instead of sausage), it was first made in the 18th century.

Jug a hare in its own blood

A jugged hare is one cooked whole, including the head, neck, ribs and liver, in a tall pot or jar. The blood is saved and added to the stew to enrich the gravy.

Red wine or port may be added, plus apples, cloves and peppercorns. For even more flavour, a bunch of herbs, including thyme, bay, parsley and marjoram, would be tied to the pot handle and immersed in the cooking liquid. Cooks of old would improvise, using large jam or pickle jars as jugs for cooking hare in this way. A jug that did not have a lid would be sealed with a pig's bladder. Whatever the receptacle, the traditional method was to seal the jar, then immerse it in a deep saucepan of simmering water so that the dish cooked very slowly and gently. Mrs Beeton advises cooking the hare in this way for 3½–4 hours, or, 'if the hare is very old', 4½ hours; she also comments that the result is 'very good'.

'First catch your hare', a phrase that has acquired proverbial status, has often been attributed to Hannah Glasse, author of The Art of Cookery Made Plain and Easy, *first published in 1747. Though she did include a recipe for jugged hare, she did not begin it with these words and would not have used a freshly killed animal: the hare would have needed to hang for a week or so before cooking.*

While the hare was cooking, the cook would prepare the essential accompaniment of fried forcemeat balls, which were made from breadcrumbs, lemon, thyme and onion. For serving, a white napkin would be tied around the jug before it was brought to the table along with the forcemeat balls, redcurrant jelly and toast.

Hares are wild game animals that have never been bred specifically for the table. However, remnants of bones found in Greece suggest that they have been enjoyed as food since around 20,000 BC. By medieval times people were eating 'hare in worts', a dish of hare with leaf vegetables. The jugged hare is probably a variation on the French *civet de lièvre*, a stew thickened with the creature's blood.

The rich, strong flavour of hare makes it an ideal soup ingredient, and hare soup is another old favourite, especially in Scotland. The parts of the animal less suited to roasting, such as the legs, are used for this dish, and the blood is also added for thickening. When roasted, the meat, because it contains little fat, needs to be larded and basted frequently during cooking.

Blood is used in many cuisines, either in sausages such as black pudding or to thicken and enrich sauces and stews. In Hungary when a pig is killed the blood is eaten straight away, fried with onions. And according to Marco Polo, Mongolian horsemen could ride for ten days without food or drink, surviving by drinking blood from the veins of their own horses.

A HAPPY HEN IS A TASTY HEN

And almost certainly a hen – or chicken – that has been reared free range in the open air rather than in intensive broiler house conditions. Now abundantly available, tender chicken was once a luxury. Most ordinary cooks of a century ago would have been happy to have an old, tougher fowl, which would have been boiled in a pot to feed their family.

Concerns over the way in which chickens are produced for the table are nothing new. In 1861, Mrs Beeton railed against the practice of fattening fowls. 'The poor birds,' she says, 'immured in their dark dungeons, ignorant that there is life and sunshine abroad, tuck their heads under their wings and make a long night of it . . . Tender, delicate, and nutritious *flesh* is the great aim; and these qualities, I can affirm without fear of contradiction, were never attained by a dungeon-fattened chicken.'

When roasting a bird of any size, old recipe books advised wrapping it in oiled paper to keep in the juices, the equivalent of the modern foil method. For boiling, a fowl would be wrapped in a floured cotton cloth, with some slices of lemon laid over the breast to keep it moist and white.

Today virtually all the chickens we cook are young birds, 1–2kg (2–4½lb) in weight, or poussins weighing around 450g (1lb). Even at Christmas it is quite rare, except on specialist farms, to find a capon – a castrated cockerel weighing 2.75–3.5kg (6–8lb), but these older birds have a good flavour.

CHICKEN IN MANY FORMS

Because of its relative blandness, chicken is the starting point for a huge variety of dishes, including:

Chicken à la king – diced chicken, mushrooms, green peppers and pimientos in a cream sherry sauce, served on toast. Probably created around the end of the 19th century by George Greenwald of the Brighton Beach Hotel, New York, for the owners, Mr and Mrs E. Clark King II.

Chicken Kiev – boned chicken rolled around herb or garlic butter, then dipped in egg and breadcrumbs and fried. Invented in the 18th century by the pioneer of food canning Nicolas Appert and enjoyed by Empress Elizabeth Petrovna of Russia, a devotee of French foods and fashions.

Chicken Marengo – chicken cooked slowly with tomatoes, garlic, parsley, white wine and cognac, seasoned with pepper and served with fried eggs (and originally with crayfish) and toast or croutons. Named for the battle in 1800 at which Napoleon defeated the Austrians; this was the dish cooked for him immediately after his victory with the ingredients that came to hand.

Coq au vin – a rustic French casserole made with a male bird and good red wine, onions, garlic and mushrooms. In an authentic version some of the blood is added to the pan. Probably originally cooked by the Gauls.

Country captain – an American version of East Indian curried chicken, said to have been brought from India to South Carolina (where the accompanying rice was grown) by a sea captain in the 1700s.

Coronation chicken – cold chicken in a curry sauce, usually with sultanas and apricots, devised for the coronation of Elizabeth II on 2 June 1953.

Choose young birds for roasting, old ones for braising

This is good advice for cooking any kind of poultry, or game birds such as pheasant and partridge, since their meat inevitably gets tougher as they age. Country folk once caught and ate many more kinds of birds than are consumed today.

Of all the game birds, pheasant are among the tastiest, whether roasted or braised. In Britain they are in season from 15 October to 1 February and are traditionally sold in a brace of one male and one (smaller) female. Out of season, cock pheasants would also be eaten in summer, when they were caught to stop them eating peas growing in cottage gardens. To catch them it was said that you should make a paper cone and smear it 'inside with treacle or gum put a few raisins in the bottom and prop the bag amongst the peas. When he sticks his head in he cannot see where to go, so he stands still till you fetch him.'

Pigeons are also scourges of crops and are shot and eaten all year round. The breasts, if plump, are tasty, but for roasting they need barding with bacon. Otherwise, they braise well, flavoured with onions and sweet herbs, and with cabbage added to the pot. They also make tasty pies, which are even better if the meat is mixed with beef and bacon.

The grouse shooting season begins in Britain on the 'Glorious Twelfth' of August, with birds being flown down from the Scottish moors to London restaurants where they are roasted and served with bread sauce.

The disadvantage of this haste is that it allows no time for hanging. For 'sportsman's grouse', birds hung for a fortnight are stuffed with butter and either rowan berries or Scottish wild raspberries. As the bird roasts, the fruit and butter cook and meld to produce a delicious sauce. Barding will improve the flavour of any roast grouse.

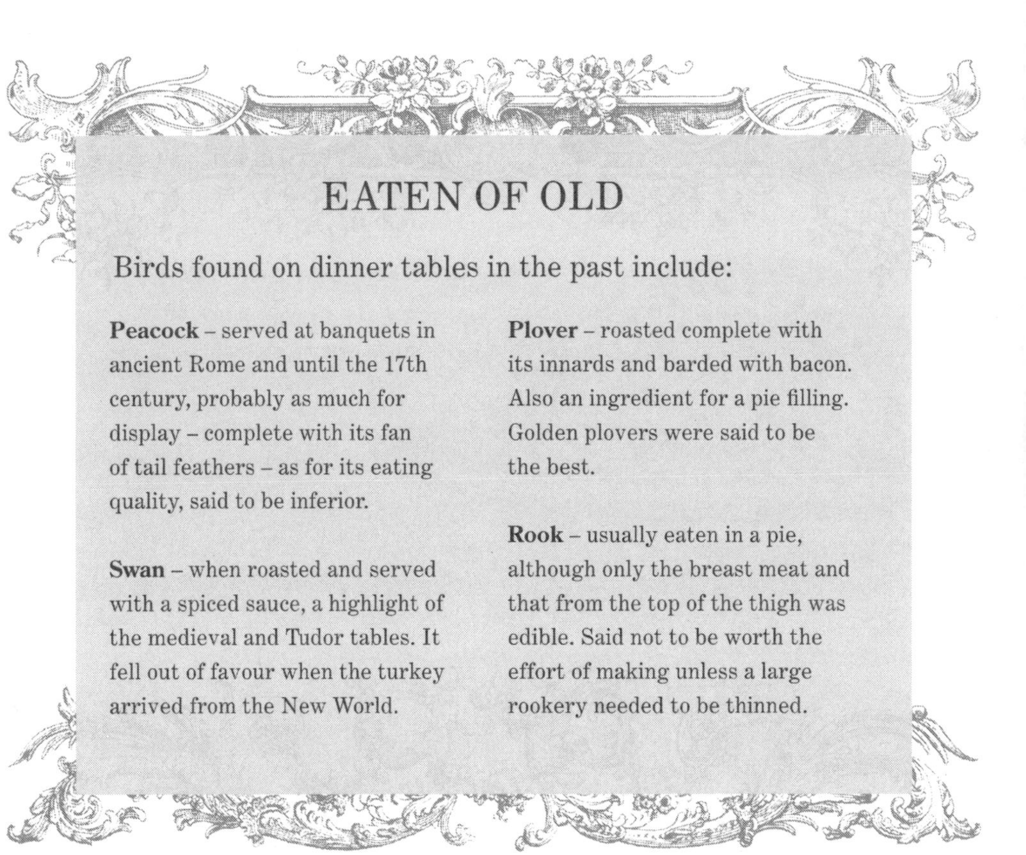

EATEN OF OLD

Birds found on dinner tables in the past include:

Peacock – served at banquets in ancient Rome and until the 17th century, probably as much for display – complete with its fan of tail feathers – as for its eating quality, said to be inferior.

Swan – when roasted and served with a spiced sauce, a highlight of the medieval and Tudor tables. It fell out of favour when the turkey arrived from the New World.

Plover – roasted complete with its innards and barded with bacon. Also an ingredient for a pie filling. Golden plovers were said to be the best.

Rook – usually eaten in a pie, although only the breast meat and that from the top of the thigh was edible. Said not to be worth the effort of making unless a large rookery needed to be thinned.

Before cooking, weigh a turkey with its stuffing

The best way of calculating the cooking time for a turkey, to make sure it will be thoroughly done. For the stuffing, chestnuts are traditional. For feasts of the past a turkey would sometimes be 'truffled' with a stuffing of truffles, mushrooms, onions, parsley and thyme fried in butter and inserted between the skin and flesh of the breast.

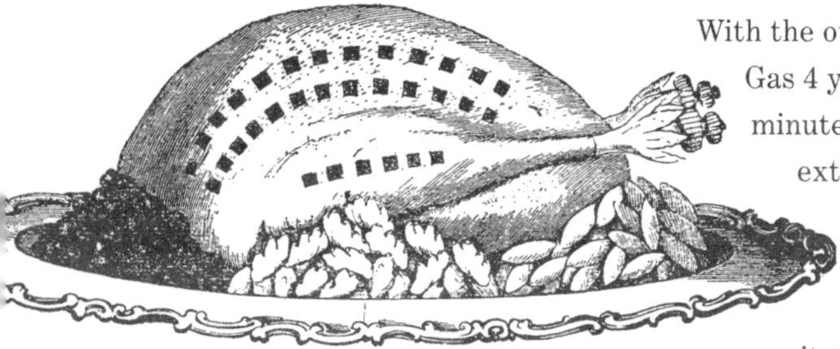

With the oven set at 180°C/350°F/ Gas 4 you need to allow 40 minutes per 450g (1lb), plus an extra 20 minutes. Cooking the bird breast side down until the last 40 minutes will help keep it moist. Until this point it can be loosely wrapped in foil if you wish. For flavour there is little to beat the Kelly Bronze – said to be the Rolls Royce of turkeys – a Norfolk Black, or any organic free-range bird.

Turkeys, bred from wild flocks native to Central America, were probably first domesticated during the 2nd millennium BC. The Aztecs considered the *huexolotlin,* as they called it, so important that they dedicated two religious festivals a year to the bird. In 1519, Cortez and his Spanish Conquistadors had found the Aztecs raising *huexolotlin* around their homes and may have been served turkey *mole poblano,* a dish prepared with chocolate and chilli. The Spaniards soon began exporting turkeys back to Europe, where they quickly became a popular choice for state banquets and other grand occasions. In 1549, some 66 turkeys were served at a banquet for Catherine de Medici.

By the 17th century turkeys had become common European farmyard birds, and from August each year they were driven from English country districts into London. Gradually they became Christmas birds, replacing goose on the menu. In the Victorian kitchen, the turkey was stuffed with forcemeats made with breadcrumbs, to which were added ingredients such as minced oysters, onions and herbs, sausage meat or minced ham, or the bird's own giblets, bound with egg yolk or whole egg.

An old name for a roast turkey garnished with a string of sausages is an 'alderman in chains'.

In North America turkey is the traditional choice for the Thanksgiving meal. It was certainly served at the second ever Thanksgiving dinner in 1623 and may also have been the centrepiece of the inaugural event in 1621, accompanied by cranberries.

In the days when they were eaten older and much less tender than their modern counterparts, turkeys would be boiled, stewed or casseroled rather than roasted. Turkey patties and pies were also popular. For keeping, the meat might even be soused in a similar way to mackerel (see page 73).

Dry a duck with hot air

A saying that relates to the Chinese tradition of making Peking duck by pumping a bird with hot air between the skin and the body before it is hung up, dipped in boiling water to blanch it and covered with maltose. In the domestic kitchen, getting the skin of a duck thoroughly dry by leaving the bird in the air for several hours will help to guarantee a beautifully crispy skin.

Peking duck, which is traditionally roasted in a vertical oven so that all the fat can drip out and the meat become tender and flaky, is one of the world's favourite duck dishes, normally served with plum sauce, chopped cucumber and spring onions (scallions) and rolled in pancakes. The Chinese first domesticated the duck some 2,000 years ago, but it was also popular in ancient Rome. The bird was plunged into boiling water before roasting to help get rid of some of the fat, and was also boiled and braised with herbs and vegetables.

The degree to which the meat is cooked is a matter of taste. The modern trend, as in France in the 1870s, is for duck to be served pink. Commenting unfavourably on this, E. S. Dallas says: 'Perhaps one of the reasons for the dissatisfaction which roast duck gives in France is that it is roasted at all, like the wild duck – very much underdone . . . a duckling will take at least half an hour of a brisk fire; a duck perhaps an hour.'

In country districts ducks were raised in the yard and were even provided with hay-filled boxes inside the house. It was the job of the housewife and children to ensure that the birds were well cared for.

DUCK DISHES

Some famous duck dishes:

Caneton à la rouennaise – after roasting, the duck breasts are carved and the carcass and liver pressed to extract the juices, which go into a flambéed sauce. The recipe dates from 1890.

Caneton à l'orange – a braised or roasted duck served with a bigarade sauce made with sour Seville orange. The dish is garnished with slices of a carefully peeled orange. The sauce is probably a French invention of the 19th century.

Caneton aux navets – duck part roasted then braised with young turnips and flavoured with herbs. A combination from medieval times.

Confit of duck – duck treated with salt and cooked and cooled under its own fat, in which state it will keep well. An old way of preserving meat.

THE ART OF CARVING IS POORLY UNDERSTOOD

But it is an art worth perfecting, for meat that is badly carved not only looks unappetizing but tastes inferior to that expertly cut from a joint or bird. Good, swift carving will also ensure that everyone is served meat that is piping hot.

The carving of a roasted, sacrificed animal and the sharing of its meat was an important ritual for people such as the ancient Greeks. Portions of the highest quality were served to those of superior status, and the liver, heart and other offal were particularly prized. A shared meal was known as a *dais*, from a verb meaning 'to divide' or 'apportion'. Other old rituals include the habit in medieval France of swearing over the meat before it was carved.

Among the earliest manuals for carvers is one written by Vincenzo Cervio, published in Venice in 1581. It contains detailed instructions on carving birds such as pheasants and peacocks. Rather than being carved on a dish the meat was speared on a carving fork and held in the air, then cut with a carving knife so that thin slices fell on to a plate below. For the carver to allow the meat to drop from the fork was a great disgrace, and carving was a desirable professional accomplishment. Cervio asserts that, 'There are three honourable offices which great Princes usually appoint to care for the needs of their stomach: the Steward, the Cupbearer and the Carver.'

In subsequent centuries, a nobleman's education was not considered complete until he had learned to carve. In *The Young Woman's Companion* of 1811, Miss T. M. Hope remarks: 'Nothing can be more disagreeable to a person who is placed at the head of a table, and whose business it is to pay the necessary honours to guests invited, than to be defective in not being properly able to carve the different articles provided.'

With any joint containing a bone, such as a leg or shoulder, the best method of carving is generally towards the bone. With a leg of lamb two or three vertical slices can be made between each horizontal one. For a rib joint, cuts are made between the bones. For breasts of poultry, cuts need to be made parallel with the breastbone. A sharp carving knife with a long blade is essential, of course (see page 15) and, for safety, a carving fork with a retractable guard to hold the meat steady.

MORE TIPS FOR THE CARVER

Technique is all important when it comes to wielding the knife.

The carver should have plenty of room to move, however closely diners are seated.

Place the joint on a large dish with room for any discarded bones.

Remove the legs and wings before carving the breast of a duck, chicken or turkey.

For a roast sirloin, loosen the meat from the chine bone before you begin.

Slice hot meat more thickly than cold.

Cut across the grain of the meat for tender, good looking slices.

A FRESH FISH HAS BRIGHT EYES

Undoubtedly one of the key signs of a fresh fish, as are firm, plump flesh and red gills. As a rule it is sensible to avoid buying fish on a Monday if you want to be assured of supreme freshness.

It is an old proverb that fish and company stink in three days.

A fresh fish will have a clean smell. Making this point, the very first entry in the Victorian household manual *Enquire Within* includes this 'amusing conundrum', which runs: 'A man went to market and bought *two* fish. When he reached home he found they were the same as when he bought them; yet there were *three*! How was this? The answer is – He bought two mackerel and one *smelt*!'

It also pays to take heed of the season, as Francatelli noted of whitebait: 'This very delicious fish is in season during the months of June, July and August . . . Owing to the extreme delicacy of this fish and its very fragile nature, it cannot be conveyed any distance during the season without injuring its quality, neither can it be kept many hours after it has been taken.'

After being caught, some fish keep better than others. As a general but not hard and fast rule, those that live nearer the surface of the water, such as mackerel, salmon, trout and herrings, keep less well than bottom feeders such as skate, plaice and sole.

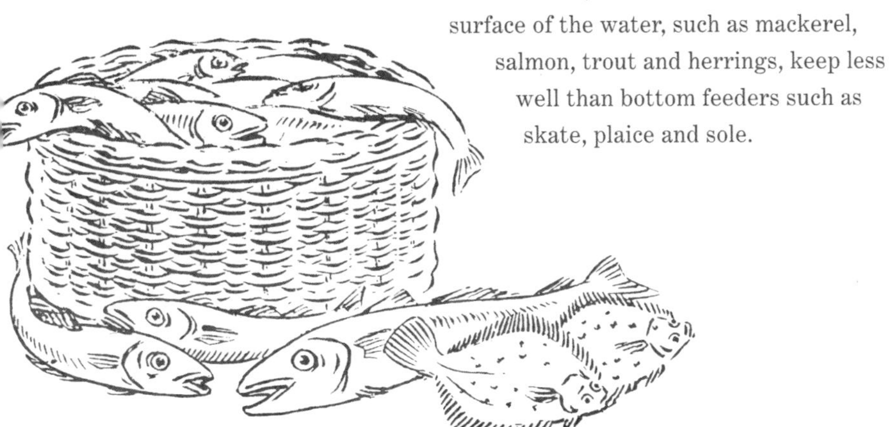

Poach a salmon in a kettle

Not the kind of kettle you would use on the stove for making a cup of tea but a large, oblong container in which a salmon – or any other large, whole fish – is cooked immersed in liquid A kettle is a name for any vessel in which liquid can be boiled.

To give a salmon plenty of flavour it needs to be poached in a *court bouillon*, a mixture of water, salt, wine, onions and other flavoursome vegetables, as well as herbs and spices. These ingredients should be boiled together for about an hour, then the liquid cooled before it is used to poach the fish. The kettle can be put on top of the stove or in a very low oven. When cooked the salmon is traditionally skinned and served cold with mayonnaise and a garnish of thinly sliced cucumber.

The salmon is the king of fish. It develops muscle as it swims upstream in search of its native river in order to spawn, having spent the winter months in its ocean feeding ground. A wild salmon caught shortly before the culmination of this homeward journey has a firm-textured flesh with more flavour and much less fat around it than that of a farmed salmon. Ideally it will be two to four years old, not a small one-year-old grilse. Salmon gets its pink colour from the pigments that accumulate as it feeds on a diet of krill, shrimp and other ocean crustaceans.

A 'pretty kettle of fish', an expression meaning a muddle, or awkward state of affairs, probably comes from the once customary and often uncomfortable riverside picnics held in the Scottish borders, at which a fire would be kindled and a newly caught salmon cooked and eaten.

SALMON OF MANY SORTS

Salmon swim into freshwater streams from both the Atlantic and the Pacific Oceans.

The Atlantic salmon, *Salmo salmar*, is fished in Northern Europe and North America, though less extensively than in past times. It makes excellent smoked salmon and gravadlax.

Pacific salmon come in various distinct species and are caught on the northern coasts of the ocean, both in North America and Asia. Best for eating are:

The sockeye, *Oncorhynchus nerka*, also called the blueback, which gets its generic name from the shape of its lower jaw (the Greek *onkos* means 'hooked'). Sockeye comes from a poor translation of *suk-kegh*, meaning 'red fish', from British Columbia's native Coast Salish language Its succulent bright orange meat is highly prized.

The chinook or spring salmon, *O. tshawytscha*, has dark spots on its tail and dorsal (upper back) fins. Its excellence has given it the alternative name of king salmon.

The chum salmon, *O. keta*, is called the dog salmon from the large canine type teeth the male fish develop at spawning time.

The coho or silver salmon, *O. kisutch*, is a deep-bodied fish that is moderately good eaten fresh but is usually canned.

PLUNGE A CRAB INTO BOILING WATER

The best way to cook a live crab – or a lobster for that matter – which also kills the creature quickly, although cooking it in a court bouillon will give it an even better flavour. It is more usual to buy a crab ready cooked, although it may still need to be properly dressed.

In Georgian Edinburgh, crab claws or 'partan's taes' were a delicacy served in taverns. *Partan* is the Gaelic term for a crab, and partan bree (crab 'brew', or soup) is a speciality of the fishing communities of north-east Scotland.

Because they are easier to catch than lobsters, crabs have been tasty fare and a source of high quality protein for ordinary folk for many centuries. Evidence of their being eaten in the west of Scotland, for instance, dates back to at least 5000 BC. Soft-shell crabs – those caught just after they have shed their old shells and before they have grown new, hard ones – are a great delicacy, especially in Venice where they are kept in baskets called *vieri* under platforms in the lagoon. To enjoy them at their best it is the custom to put the live crabs in a bowl of beaten eggs, which they eat before they drown. The crabs are then coated in flour and fried in olive oil.

Dressing a crab is a fiddly business, which is well described in *The Concise Household Encyclopedia* of 1933:

'. . . break off the large and small claws, remove the underneath portion and all the flesh from the shell, also the little bag near the head, usually full of sand, and throw away all bone and the long greyish pieces called the dead man's fingers. The flesh is of two kinds, some firm and white, the

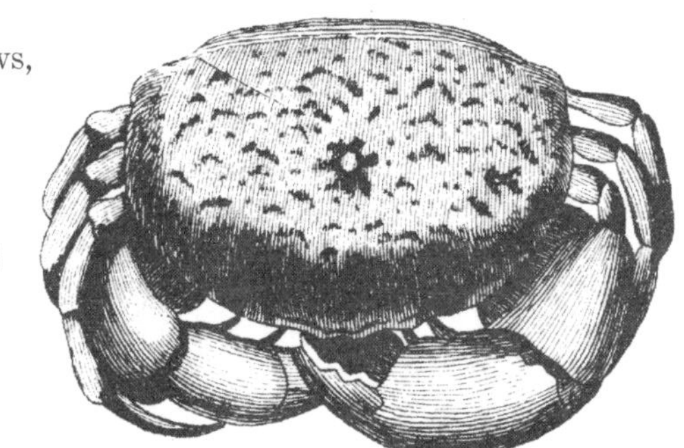

rest soft and dark. Separate the former into shreds with a fork, also the meat from the claws after cracking them. Mix the dark soft meat with about 2 tablespoonfuls each of fresh breadcrumbs and oil and vinegar and seasoning to taste. Season the shredded white meat, but keep separate from the remainder.' The meat is then returned to the washed shell, arranging white and dark portions alternately.

Worldwide, cooks have created many delicious dishes using crab as a main ingredient. Creole crab gumbo, made with okra and green peppers, has the glutinous texture typical of okra dishes. In Thai cuisine, crab cakes containing rice are flavoured with lemon grass and chilli. British favourites include potted crab, made in a similar way to potted shrimps, and gratinated crab, a hot dish containing Worcestershire sauce and mustard, topped with grated cheese and grilled.

CRABBY LANGUAGE

To catch a crab – when rowing, failure to insert the oar deeply enough, so that the rower loses balance and may even fall overboard.

Crab canon – in music a canon in which the notes of the theme are repeated by the imitating voice in reverse order. The name comes from the old belief that crabs walk backwards (though in fact they scuttle sideways).

Diogenes crab – a type of West Indian hermit crab which, like the eponymous Greek philosopher who eschewed life's amenities and lived in a tub, resides in the empty shell of another crustacean.

A GOOD LOBSTER FEELS HEAVY IN THE HAND

Because, if light, it will be watery and poor. The heaviness is an indication that there is good firm meat inside the shell. If choosing a live lobster look, too, for strong movements of the claws. Of all the dishes made with this expensive shellfish, lobster thermidor is among the most luxurious.

It is not true that lobsters squeal when put into boiling water – it is impossible since they have no vocal cords. The noise comes from the rapid contraction of the segments of their shells.

As well as weight, there are other considerations to take into account, as Dolby's *Cook's Dictionary* of 1833 makes clear: 'When you buy them ready boiled, try whether their tails are stiff and pull up with a spring, otherwise that part will be flabby. The cock lobster may be distinguished from the hen by the narrow back part of the tail, and the two uppermost fins within it are stiff and hard; but those of the hen are soft, and the tail broader.' While the smaller males have a better flavour, hen lobsters are prized for their coral (the massed eggs), which are valued for sauces, particularly for colouring mayonnaise. A freshly cooked lobster needs little more than a good hollandaise or simply melted butter for total enjoyment – as well as crackers to break into the claws, a large napkin to protect your clothes and a finger bowl for cleaning your hands.

Lobster thermidor was created in 1894 by Marie's, a Paris restaurant near the Comédie Française, to honour the opening of the play *Thermidor* by Victorien Sardou. In the French Republican calendar, Thermidor was the second month of the summer quarter; the word means 'heat'. The play – about the overthrow of Robespierre – was soon forgotten, but the dish found lasting fame. It consists of cooked lobster meat mixed with cream, egg yolks and brandy or sherry, stuffed into a lobster shell, topped with grated Parmesan cheese and browned under a hot grill (broiler). To be true to the original recipe the sauce must contain powdered mustard.

Lobster Newburg, lobster meat served with a sauce of butter, cream, eggs and sherry or Madeira wine, with some paprika or cayenne pepper added, also originated as a restaurant dish. The story goes that a ship's captain named Ben Wenberg, returning from the West Indies in 1876, demonstrated in Delmonico's Restaurant in New York his new way of serving lobster to chef Charles Ranhofer. It was soon on the menu as lobster à la Wenberg, but Wenburg had an altercation with the restaurant and although he was no longer welcome there his dish was still in demand. So the first two letters of the name were switched – hence lobster Newburg.

Mackerel are excellent if soused

That is, preserved in a mixture of vinegar and spices after cooking. Mackerel deteriorate quickly after they have been caught, and in the days before refrigeration and deep freezing, this form of marinating was a particularly good way of keeping them for a week or more.

To souse mackerel they should first be thoroughly washed and dried and the roes removed. Then just cover them with salted water and poach them for 20–30 minutes until tender. Drain them, keeping the cooking liquor, and

'The mackerel has this in common with good women – he is loved by all the world.' (Grimond de la Reynère)

put them in a dish with some bay leaves, whole peppercorns, some fennel seeds and some strips of lemon zest. Discard half the poaching liquor and replace it with vinegar, and pour it over the fish, to cover. They are best if left for two or three days before being eaten and enjoyed with brown bread and butter.

Mackerel are a bargain buy, and high in health-giving omega 3 fish oils. When fresh they have a beautiful blue sheen, and some say that their name may be a diminutive of 'nacre', another name for mother of pearl. In some parts of the South of France the mackerel was once called the *poisson d'Avril*, the April fish and also an April fool – possibly for allowing itself to be caught so easily from this spring month onwards, throughout the summer.

Because they spoil so quickly mackerel were, in the 19th century, the only fish that were allowed be sold in London streets on a Sunday.

Soak anchovies in milk

If, that is, they are the salted kind, preserved in oil and bought in small, flattish tins or in jars. The milk helps to draw out the saltiness and make them more palatable.

The 'English anchovies' eaten in Victorian times were, in fact, sprats (small herrings) salted and preserved in a similar way.

The anchovies that are most often used in the kitchen are those of the species *Engraulis encrasicolus*, the European anchovy, which are found in the Mediterranean, the Black Sea and in the warmer parts of the eastern Atlantic. Since the Middle Ages, and probably

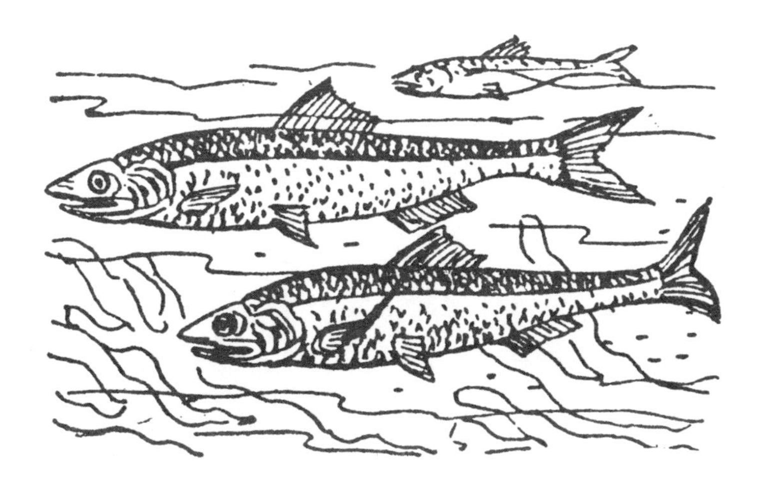

earlier, these small fish, caught between April and October, have been salted and kept in barrels. The best, which were greatly appreciated by Louis XI, are still said to come from Collioure in southern France.

Anchovies – usually but not invariably the salted kind – are a key ingredient of a *salade niçoise* and a Scandinavian snack called Jansson's temptation, which is traditionally eaten on New Year's Eve. The latter is essentially a gratin of potatoes mixed with anchovies and cream. In Provence, *anchoïade*, made from salt anchovies pounded with vinegar and mixed with chopped onions and hard-boiled egg, is spread on slices of fresh crusty bread then browned in the oven.

Mediterranean anchovies are a key ingredient of Patum Peperium or 'Gentleman's Relish', in which they are blended with butter, herbs and spices. Invented by John Osborn, an English provision merchant living in Paris in 1828, the recipe for this salty paste, which is wonderful spread on hot toast or added to scrambled eggs, remains top secret. In the 1930s it became closely associated with the British upper class.

CHAPTER 3

ALL THE BEST METHODS

In the kitchen, technique counts. Knowing how to do things properly not only prevents mistakes – and the risk of spoiling or wasting precious ingredients – but ensures that finished dishes look as good as they taste. As cooks grow in confidence, and learn how ingredients behave when stirred and whipped, heated and cooled, they inevitably, without necessarily being conscious of the fact, absorb the science as well as the art of cookery. Armed with this knowledge they can hone and expand their skills and so tackle ever more complex recipes and tasks, as well as remaining truly proficient in the simple things.

Once basic techniques have been mastered they can be applied again and again for, as the journalist and gastronome E. S. Dallas aptly remarked, 'He who has learnt to broil a steak properly does not require a special receipt for broiling a mutton chop; and he who can make half a dozen sauces has really learnt to make half a hundred . . .' The key is to experiment and to find out what works for you for, as Dallas, author of the 1877 *Kettner's Book of the Table* continues, '. . . everybody knows that vegetables are not alike in flavour. Some apples are comparatively tasteless; so are some carrots; and one lemon is sharper than another. Therefore in one kitchen a lemon, an apple, or a couple of carrots will go further to flavour a sauce than double the number in another kitchen.'

A PERFECT SANDWICH HAS NO CRUSTS

Removing the crusts is certainly necessary for creating dainty sandwiches for an afternoon tea, but is not really required for less formal occasions such as picnics.

A tried and tested tip when buttering many slices of bread for sandwiches: look after the edges and the middles will look after themselves. For fancy sandwiches, bread can be shaped with pastry or cookie cutters.

Sandwiches are said to have been invented in 1762, when John Montagu, Earl of Sandwich, asked for meat and bread to be brought to him at the gaming table so as to avoid interrupting his pleasure. Once the sandwich was accepted, other ingredients were quickly added, and the technique perfected.

This 1886 description of the Bretby sandwich from Charles Elmé Francatelli is typical: 'First cut some thin slices of white bread and butter; then, cover half of these, first, with finely-shred white heart lettuce, then with very thin slices of roast or boiled fowl; these to be placed alternately side by side with fillets of anchovies; strew some shredded lettuce over this, place a slice of bread and butter over the whole, and after slightly pressing the sandwich with the blade of a knife, proceed to cut the preparation into oblong shapes, about two and a half inches long, by one in width.'

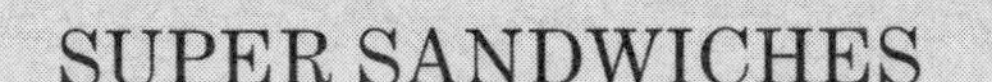

SUPER SANDWICHES

The club sandwich – a double decker sandwich that possibly originated on the twin-decker club cars of American streamliner trains of the late 19th century. It is also attributed to the Saratoga Club in New York, where in 1894 Richard Canfield, an art patron who had bought the club, turned it into a gaming venue and invented the double decker to serve to his clientele.

The Dagwood – a large sandwich named for the American comic strip character Dagwood Bumstead. The sandwich, which was small at first but later became a colossal mouthful, first appeared in *Blondie* on 16 April 1936.

Po'boy or poorboy – a New Orleans speciality of well cooked meat, thickly sliced and served with a rich gravy in a split French loaf with mayonnaise, tomatoes and shredded lettuce. Named for its low price and good value.

MELBA TOAST NEEDS COOKING TWICE

This very thin, crisp dry toast is made by lightly toasting a thick slice of bread, cutting it in half horizontally, then toasting it again.

Melba toast is named for the great Australian opera singer Helen Porter Mitchell, whose stage name was Nellie Melba. It is said that in 1897, when she was staying at the Ritz Hotel in Paris, she fell ill, and the chef Auguste Escoffier (who had previously invented the *pêche Melba* in her honour while working at the Savoy in London) created this toast, which she much enjoyed, to aid her recovery. The invention of the name is attributed to the hotel's owner, César Ritz, although it was originally named for his wife Marie Ritz.

The history of toast is probably as old as bread itself, but 'tost' was certainly popular in the Middle Ages when pieces of bread were toasted before being put in soups or used to mop up gravy. At this time cooks also made 'pokerounce' – toast topped with hot honey, ginger, cinnamon and galangal. By the 16th century everything from poached eggs to bacon, cheese and anchovies was being served on toast, and within another century cinnamon toast – made by covering the toast with a mixture of cinnamon sugar and wine – was all the rage.

Toast, served with marmalade, is a part of the quintessential English breakfast. In Italy, *bruschette*, thick slices of toast rubbed with garlic, dressed with virgin olive oil and scattered with salt, are traditionally eaten at the beginning of a meal. The bruschetta, which originated in Lazio and Abruzzo, was originally intended as a means of showing off the results of the new season's oil harvest but is now served in many different ways, and with everything from tomatoes to chopped wild fennel and cannellini beans.

French toast is not toast at all but bread dipped in beaten egg and milk and fried in butter. It can be savoury or sweet.

The colder the dish, the more seasoning it needs

A good reason for cooks to taste as they cook, and to be generous with salt, pepper, herbs and spices in dishes that are to be served cold, chilled or frozen.

Making the right judgements on such seasoning comes with experience. In hot dishes, the aromatic oils and other volatile chemicals that seasonings contain are more readily released and stimulate both the smell receptors in the nose and the taste buds, so enhancing flavour. With cold food, the taste buds do not have this olfactory back-up. An example of a cold dish that needs to be highly seasoned is a brawn, also known as head cheese. This dish was made in medieval times from the head of a wild boar, and was a dish traditionally served as part of a Christmas feast. Unlike the modern version, the meat was not set in jelly but kept in a pot of pickling liquor.

To have a good flavour when cold the mixture for a brawn needs to have so much salt and pepper in it as to be virtually unpalatable when hot.

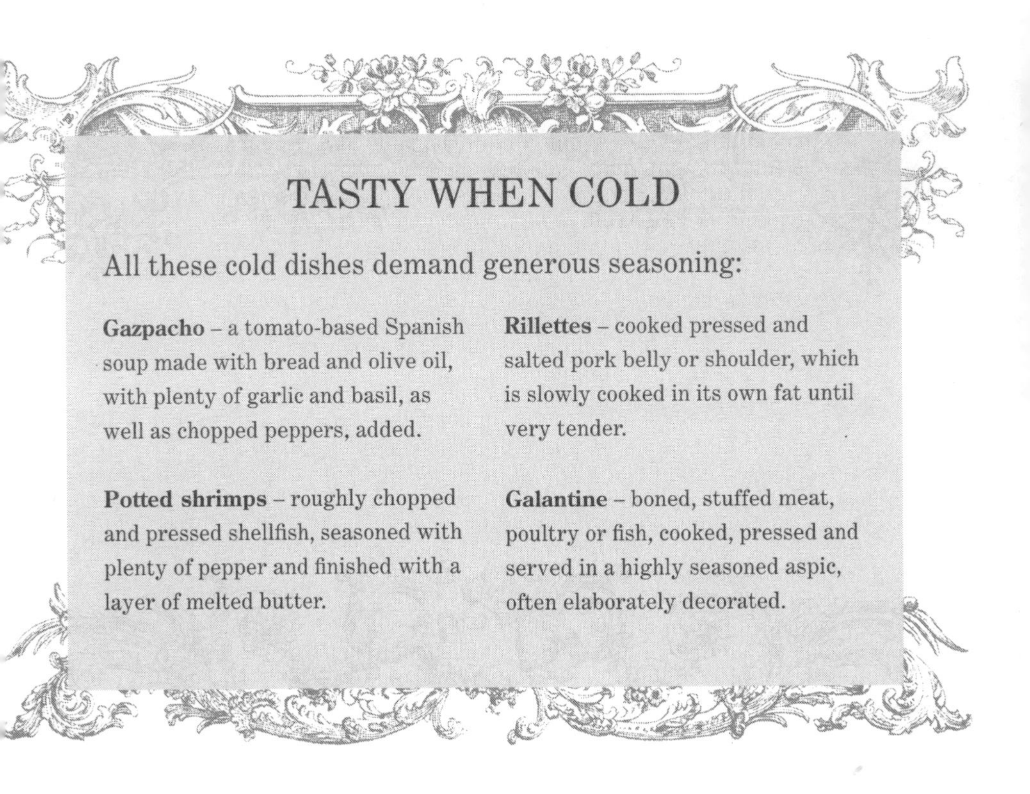

TASTY WHEN COLD

All these cold dishes demand generous seasoning:

Gazpacho – a tomato-based Spanish soup made with bread and olive oil, with plenty of garlic and basil, as well as chopped peppers, added.

Potted shrimps – roughly chopped and pressed shellfish, seasoned with plenty of pepper and finished with a layer of melted butter.

Rillettes – cooked pressed and salted pork belly or shoulder, which is slowly cooked in its own fat until very tender.

Galantine – boned, stuffed meat, poultry or fish, cooked, pressed and served in a highly seasoned aspic, often elaborately decorated.

If the soup is too salty, add sugar

This trick, which works especially well for tomato soup, is also effective for gravy. The sugar seems to neutralize the taste of the salt, possibly because these two basic flavours are sensed on different parts of the tongue.

Another good tip is to put a sliced potato into soup that is too salty, then remove and discard it before serving; the vegetable will absorb a lot of the excess salt. Adding milk can help, too, but this is a possibility only if the soup already has milk or cream as one of its ingredients.

When eating soup, says Judith Martin, America's Miss Manners, etiquette demands that it 'should always be kept flowing in the opposite direction from one's lap. The soup spoon should be filled from its far side and the soup poured gently into the mouth with its near side.'

Soup is one of the oldest foods and for centuries it consisted of either bread soaked in broth or broth poured over bread. Only from the 1800s was it served without the bread or 'sops'. Soups made from game animals and birds were staples in the diet of early American pioneers. In 1837 Miss Leslie in her *Directions for Cookery, in its Various Branches* advised: '. . . be careful to proportion the amount of water to the amount of meat. Somewhat less than a quart to a pound of meat is a good rule for common soups. Rich soups, intended for company, may have a still smaller allowance for water.'

French fries should be twice cooked

A sure way of getting good results, whether the potatoes are parboiled before frying or fried twice, and whatever name you give them.

Large fries are what the British call chips. To Americans chips are very thin, oval pieces of fried potato; these are described on British menus as game chips and are sold ready salted and flavoured as crisps.

The idea of cooking potatoes twice when making fries is to get the insides soft and the outsides really crisp. Potatoes can be parboiled whole or in good-sized chunks before being cooled, cut and deep fried, but an even better method is this. First cut them to size then soak them in cold water for at least two hours to help get rid of some of the starch. Ideally, says the *Constance Spry Cookery Book*, they should be 40–50mm (2–2½in) long and 6–12mm (¼–½in) thick. Dry them well, then deep fry them in oil heated to 150°C (300°F) for about six minutes, until they are soft to the touch. Take them out and drain them on paper towels to remove excess oil then fry them again at the higher temperature of 180°C (360°F) for two or three minutes. Finally, sprinkle them with salt.

French fries are also known as pommes Pont Neuf because street vendors sold them on this bridge in Paris.

The custom of deep frying elongated potato pieces probably came not from France but from Belgium. It is said that in the 1680s the inhabitants of the Meuse Valley between Dinant and Liège would, when they had no small fried fish to accompany their meals, cut up potatoes and fry them as substitutes. Some time between 1801 and 1809 a manuscript written by Thomas Jefferson records '*pommes de terres frites à cru en petites tranches*' (literally 'potatoes deep fried while raw, cut into small pieces'), a recipe that almost certainly came from his French chef, Honoré Julien.

For game chips, the traditional accompaniment to venison and game birds such as pheasant and grouse, the potatoes need to be cut into very fine slices, ideally with a mandolin. They are soaked in cold water and dried, then fried in very hot oil at 200°C 395°F) for a minute or two until they rise to the surface and are golden brown.

POTATO LORE AND CUSTOM

It is said that:

If a woman is expecting a baby, she should not eat potatoes because the baby will be born with a big head.

If a man dislikes a woman but can't tell her so to her face he should peel a potato and put the peel on her doorstep on May Day.

Keep a potato in your pocket to cure rheumatism and eczema.

If you want to get rid of a wart, rub it with a cut potato, then bury the potato in the ground. As the potato rots in the ground, your wart will disappear.

In cases of toothache, the advice is to carry a peeled potato in a pocket on the same side as the bad tooth. As the potato falls apart the tooth will heal.

SKIN TOMATOES WITH EASE: POUR ON BOILING WATER

By far the best way of skinning tomatoes, and also fruit such as peaches and nectarines. Skinned, disgorged tomatoes are essential for achieving smooth sauces.

Tomatoes are among the most versatile of ingredients, and there are few summer tastes better than outdoor ripened fruit. In winter, however, canned skinned plum tomatoes are a better option for flavour than insipid fresh ones, and you can always add a little tomato paste for a deeper taste. All good cooks have in their repertoires their own versions of tomato sauce, tomato salad and soups hot and cold.

The tomato (*Lycopersicon lycopersicum*), a native of the Americas, was first cultivated by the Aztecs who named it *tomatl*, meaning 'plump fruit'. In Europe, the Spanish and Italians were first to take to the tomato with relish, and the first tomato recipe, for 'Tomato sauce, Spanish style', appeared in a Neapolitan book of the 1690s by one Antonio Latini; it is therefore no accident that tomato sauce has a particular affinity with pasta. However the fruit was greeted with great suspicion when it first arrived from

The tomato's tag of 'love apple' comes from its 16th-century reputation as an aphrodisiac, hence the Latin *poma amoris*, the French *pomme d'amour* and the Italian *pomodoro*.

across the Atlantic, possibly because of its resemblance to the red berries of its poisonous relative the woody nightshade (*Solanum dulcamara*).

This attitude towards the tomato remained prevalent in Britain until the 19th century. Writing in 1945 of her country childhood, Flora Thompson, author of *Lark Rise to Candleford*, records these comments of hamlet folk: '. . . nasty sour things, they be, as only gentry can eat,' and 'Don't 'ee go tryin' to eat it now . . . It'll only make 'ee sick. I know because I had one of the nasty horrid things at our Minnie's.'

RICE MUST BE PLUNGED INTO BOILING WATER AND FINISHED IN THE SAME WAY

Sound advice from one Colonel Kenney Herbert, alias 'Wyvern', writing in the early 20th century about boiling rice for curry. Cooks of the period were unanimous that the grains of cooked rice should always be separated with a fork, never a spoon.

The tradition of throwing rice over a bride stems from an old Hindu ritual, in which rice is a symbol of fruitfulness.

Whether the rice should be washed before cooking was a moot point. The Colonel was adamant that rice for the English market was 'so carefully refined and winnowed' that it should not. The English cook Eliza Acton, writing half a century earlier, strongly recommends pre-washing, but finishes her cooking by leaving rice in a colander to drain in a warm place for ten minutes.

Some dishes demand a different approach. For a risotto (see page 27) the secret is for the rice to absorb all the liquid and flavour of a good stock. A plump medium-grain variety such as arborio, grown in northern Italy, from where risotto originates, is the authentic choice. In a Middle Eastern pilaf the rice is washed, and may be soaked overnight, before being boiled, then steamed until *mufalfal*, with every grain perfectly separate and tender.

Rice pudding has its origins as a dessert in the Middle Ages, when cooked rice was mixed with almond or cows' milk and sweetened. Before this, rice and milk was a pottage for invalids. The Victorians made elaborate dishes, both sweet and savoury, beginning with rice moulded into a ring.

ALWAYS PEEL ONIONS UNDER WATER

Immersion is good for two reasons. For large onions, cold water can stop them from making you cry. For small pickling onions or shallots, boiling water loosens stubborn skins and eases the labour of peeling.

Peeling onions makes your eyes stream because when their tissues are cut they give off pyruvic acid and allicin, volatile substances called lachrymators. When these meet the fluid in the eye they create a weak – but stinging – solution. Under cold running water, the lachrymators have the chance of dissolving before they can get to the eyes. For slicing and chopping, however, there is no alternative to bearing the pain, but it may help to cool the onions in the refrigerator for an hour or two before you need them; this makes the lachrymators a little less volatile.

The fiery chemical components of onions are quickly and easily subdued by cooking. When heated, the volatile odours are dissipated and some are converted, for our pleasure, into sugar; others turn into chemicals more than

Keeping cut onions in the house has long been said to be unlucky. The reason often given was that the cut surface would absorb impurities from the air and 'breed distempers'.

fifty times sweeter. It is this sweetness that makes the tear-jerking preparation of a French onion stew so worthwhile, and onions so indispensable in the kitchen.

If you have contact lenses, wear them while preparing onions and you'll cry a lot less. Or look out for the new 'Supasweet' onions, bred to have a much lower pyruvic acid content than regular types.

To chop an onion, the best technique is to peel it, cut it in half vertically, then cut each half into very thin slices without separating them from the root. If you then make close horizontal cuts you will end up with fine dice. The root can be discarded.

A cut onion was said to have curative powers. When placed in a room with a sick child it would, some believed, 'draw the complaint to itself'. The onion was then summarily burnt.

Make meatballs with wet hands

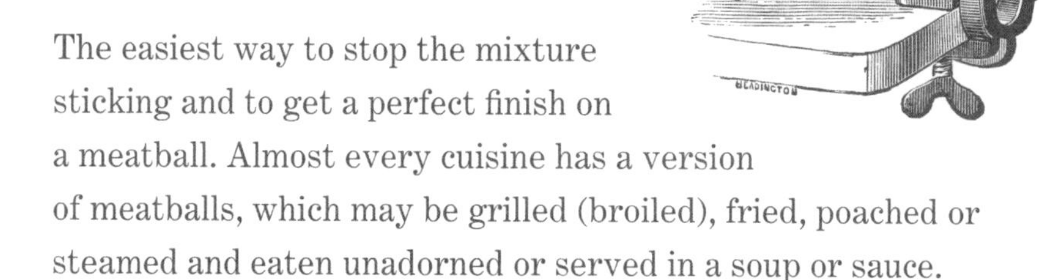

The easiest way to stop the mixture sticking and to get a perfect finish on a meatball. Almost every cuisine has a version of meatballs, which may be grilled (broiled), fried, poached or steamed and eaten unadorned or served in a soup or sauce.

Because they are frequently made with cheaper cuts of meat not good enough for roasting or grilling, from offal (variety meats), or from cooked meat left over from a previous meal, meatballs are often regarded as poor man's food but in fact are the epitome of thrift. It is usual for the meat to be bound in some way, with egg, béchamel sauce or bread soaked in milk, or a mixture of these, or with rice or some other carbohydrate. Adding bread is also a good way to make a small amount of meat go further.

Among the oldest types of British meatball are faggots or 'savoury ducks', made from minced belly pork, pigs' liver and other offal, bound with

breadcrumbs, well seasoned with chopped onion, sage, salt and pepper. For the real thing, they should then be wrapped up in pieces of caul fat (the membrane found around the intestine) before being baked. These were certainly made by 1666, for it was an accident with a batch of faggots being cooked in Pudding Lane that started the Great Fire of London.

In baseball, a meatball is a pitch that travels so slowly through the strike zone that it is easily hit.

The ancient Roman cookbook *Apicius*, probably written in the 5th century, contains recipes for faggot-like meatballs. Italian favourites of today are *polpette di carne.* Every family has its own recipe, passed down the generations. A typical mixture is minced beef, garlic, parsley, Parmesan cheese, eggs, nutmeg, salt and pepper. These are rolled in flour to coat them lightly, then fried. They are served in a clear meat stock or a tomato sauce.

MEATBALLS GALORE

Some tasty meatballs from around the world:

Lions' heads – large pork meatballs cooked in a casserole with shredded greens. A Shanghai speciality.

Frikadeller – Danish fried meatballs, made from pork and veal, with onions, salt and pepper.

Keftedes – Greek meatballs flavoured with onions and garlic and often served with a cucumber and yoghurt tzatziki.

Köfte – Turkish lamb meatballs often grilled on sticks, kebab-style.

Bakso – Indonesian meatballs, bound with tapioca flour and poached in a soup to which noodles, tofu and spring onions may be added.

Albóndigas – Mexican meatballs poached in a chicken broth. They are bound with rice and egg and flavoured with herbs such as mint.

Add vinegar to the water when you poach an egg

For the inexperienced cook, a sensible precaution to help the egg white seal quickly – lemon juice has the same effect. Too much vinegar can mar the flavour if the eggs are to be eaten plain, but will be thoroughly disguised by a sauce.

Making perfectly poached eggs is a culinary art that is worth mastering. Start with a deep frying pan filled with 7.5cm (3in) water with, if you wish, 1 or 2 tablespoons of mild vinegar added. When the water has reached a rolling boil, crack an egg into a part of the water that is bubbling hard so that it spins around in the vortex. (If you are nervous, crack the egg into a saucer first.) Add more eggs in the same way, then lower the heat to get the gentlest of simmers. After about four minutes the whites should be set and the yolks still runny. Lift the cooked eggs out of the water with a slotted spoon and trim away any untidy white.

Eggs Benedict – an English muffin topped with grilled Canadian bacon (not cold ham), poached eggs, hollandaise sauce and (for sheer luxury) a slice of truffle – has been an American favourite for decades. There are various versions of its origin. One is that Mrs LeGrand Benedict devised it, in conjunction with the chef at New York's Delmonico's Restaurant, in the 1860s. Another is that in 1894 it was ordered by Lemuel Benedict, a Wall Street broker, when suffering from a hangover. A New Orleans speciality is eggs Sardou – poached eggs with spinach, artichoke hearts, anchovies, chopped ham, truffles and

Poaching works well for any food that needs gentle cooking. The word comes from the French *pocher*, meaning pocket, and refers specifically to the pocket of liquid yolk within the set white of a poached egg.

hollandaise. It was created for the French playwright Victorien Sardou at Antoine's Restaurant in the 1870s.

The fresher the eggs, the better the white of a poached egg will set. But never add salt to the water as it will break up the white. Less confident cooks can poach their eggs in the cups or rings of a poacher, but unless this allows them to be totally immersed in the simmering water, the resulting eggs are essentially coddled, not poached.

Whisk egg whites in a copper bowl

For a stable foam that can be whisked stiff and will stay firm and not collapse, there is nothing to surpass a copper bowl, but a clean, dry container, whatever it is made of, is essential to a good result.

One of the problems of beating egg whites stiff, particularly for making meringues, is that if overbeaten they separate out into a nasty mess of lumps and liquid. What cooks of the past discovered by trial and error has now been proved in the laboratory: a reaction between conalbumin (one of the proteins in the white) and copper prevents the foam from separating and imparts a creamy yellow colour quite different from the snowy white of a foam whisked in a glass, stainless steel or ceramic bowl.

Pure egg white is essential to a good result. Just a drop of yolk in the bowl can reduce the volume of beaten egg white by over 60 per cent, and particles of oil or grease can have a similar, though less

Dropping egg white into water (all of it, or a few drops from an egg pricked with a pin) and interpreting the shape created is an old method of divination. Gypsies are reported to have 'seen' everything from ships to churches and coffins using this method.

drastic effect. If you have a copper bowl, keep it spotless. Rub off any green patches of potentially harmful copper oxide with a mixture of salt and lemon juice, then wash and dry it thoroughly before use. Salt makes whites hard to whip and decreases their stability.

SKIN FISH FROM TAIL TO HEAD

The best way of removing the skin from most fish before it is cooked, except for whiting and haddock, which need the opposite treatment. You also need a sharp knife and a firm, decisive action. If not skinned, a whole fish or a large fillet may benefit from being de-scaled.

For skinning a fish a filleting knife or a fairly narrow-bladed cook's knife is ideal. You first need to make an incision between flesh and skin, then (if you are right handed), hold the skin tightly in your left hand and, with a swift action of the knife in your right, take the skin off completely. A word of warning: if the fish is very fresh, do not work so quickly that the flesh is torn.

Writing in 1860 in The Dinner Question, *'Tabitha Tickletooth' thought filleting unnecessary, at least for a fish such as a sole. 'This is a French method,' she says, 'pursued in clubs and large establishments; but for homely kitchens it will be found extravagant.'*

To descale a fish, lay it on a board with its head towards you, hold it firmly by the tail and, with the blunt side of the knife, scrape vigorously against the grain of the scales. Wipe the knife and repeat until the skin is smooth, then wash and dry the fish. Soak fish in water for half an hour to make its scales easier to remove.

The confident cook will also be able to fillet a fish. The essentials are to cut off the head and fins and to make a cut across the tail. Then, with the fish placed on a board, make a cut down the spine. Working from the spine outwards, and with the knife pressed against the bones, make long even cuts to remove the fillets.

Shape quenelles with two spoons

The easiest way of creating neat shapes for these small but delicate dumplings made with finely minced (ground) meat or fish and bound with egg. Breadcrumbs may also be included. It is said that the only way in which pike can be properly enjoyed is in the dish *quenelles de brochet*.

Serve pike quenelles on rounds of toast and, for a classic accompaniment, surround them with a lobster, shrimp or white wine sauce.

Quenelles may be served as a starter or fish course, or added to a soup or a fine stew. Lady Agnes Jekyll, in her *Kitchen Essays* of 1922, recommends giving a consommé distinction by finishing each bowl with a quenelle 'of cream of chicken, moulded the size of a dessert spoon, with a few peas or vegetables reduced almost to a glaze, placed in the centre of the quenelle, and covered with a little more chicken cream, and poached lightly in water, kept hot, and one slipped into each portion . . .'

In *quenelles de brochet* minced raw pike is mixed with egg whites, lemon juice and cream then moulded between two spoons before being poached in stock. For thickening, some cooks

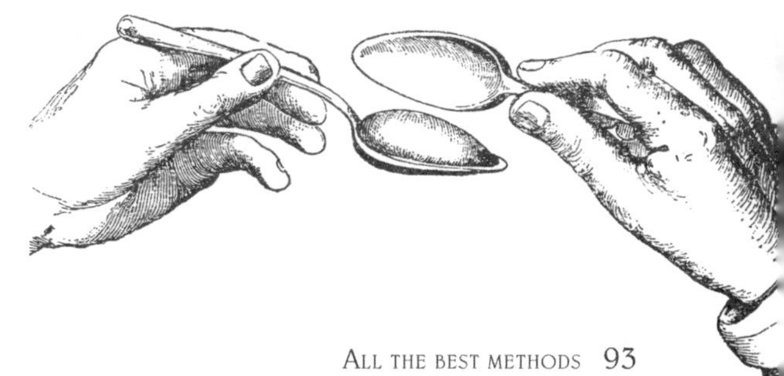

also add a panada or panade made by boiling 250ml (½ pint) water with 25g (1oz) butter and a pinch of salt, then adding four large tablespoons of flour and cooking the mixture for about five minutes until it is thick and smooth.

Remove citrus zest with a potato peeler

A reasonable means of getting strips of zest without the bitter pith attached, but for a finer result it is best to use a zester or, in the 21st-century kitchen, a super-sharp microplane grater. The intense flavour of the zest comes from the aromatic oils it contains.

If a woman wants to know whether she will get the man she desires it is said she should put a lemon peel in each armpit and keep them there all day. Before going to bed she must rub the bedposts with them. If she is in luck the man she fancies will come to her in a dream.

The addition of citrus zest makes all the difference to the flavour of a dish, but before you zest it is wise to choose unwaxed fruit and to wash and dry it thoroughly to remove any dyes or pesticides that may have been sprayed on to it. A zester is a device shaped rather like a potato peeler but instead of a slit it has about five holes in the top. To make it work well you do have to apply considerable pressure, and the strips it produces may still need to be finely chopped before you use them. To get finely grated zest easily there is nothing to beat the microplane grater, whose dozens of small blades deliver the zest in seconds flat.

An old recipe for a quick and simple lemonade is to simmer the thinly pared rind of a lemon with three tablespoons of water for 20 minutes, then add the strained juice of the fruit. This is even nicer when added to gin or vodka.

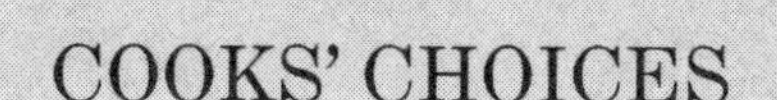

COOKS' CHOICES

Each variety of citrus fruit has a subtly different flavour, which will affect the cook's selection of zest, flesh and juice.

Lemon – very versatile and ideal for both sweet and savoury dishes, from a lemon mousse to flavouring a stuffing for a chicken. Whole lemons, complete with zest and pith, are preserved in salt and used in Middle Eastern dishes.

Orange – the zest will enliven any chocolate dessert and add a distinctive flavour to braised vegetables such as red cabbage. Orange hybrids, such as the mandarin and tangerine, also have distinctive flavours. Both the zest and the pith of bitter Seville oranges are essential for making marmalade (see page 139).

Lime – an important ingredient in Thai cooking and also in desserts such as key lime pie, which should be made, for authenticity, with the small, sour, key limes native to the tropics. They are so named because they grow on the islands of the Florida Keys.

Grapefruit – even without pith it has a strong, slightly bitter flavour, but is good for desserts and, with its pith attached, ideal for marmalade.

Kumquat – the zest of this miniature orange fruit is usually eaten as part of the whole fruit, which can be enjoyed fresh, candied or preserved.

Ugli – a huge fruit with a baggy rind and sweet, lemony-flavoured flesh. A grapefruit–mandarin hybrid.

To save separated mayonnaise, add another egg

The sound advice of the 19th-century American perfectionist Fannie Merritt Farmer and many good cooks before and since, although hot water is also recommended by some.

The writer Alice Thomas Ellis maintained that 'mayonnaise proves the existence of God,' and that 'an angel must have divulged that recipe and then explained what to do with the left-over whites.' Mayonnaise is made by adding oil drop by drop to egg yolks mixed with some salt, while beating vigorously and continuously. As you mix, the oil is broken into smaller and smaller droplets, which eventually stabilize into a rich, thick emulsion. Adding the oil too fast, or insufficient beating, are usually what makes the mixture separate out, so that pools of oil form, making the mayonnaise look curdled. Keeping cool is, in every sense, critical to the process (and the sanity of the cook), because it makes everything more stable.

Mayonnaise was probably named from Port Mahon, the capital of the Balearic island Minorca, by the chef of the Duc de Richelieu, to commemorate the duke's taking of the island in 1756.

'Smooth consistency,' says Miss Farmer, 'may be restored by taking the yolk of another egg and adding curdled mixture to it.' And, she adds, 'it is desirable to have bowl containing mixture placed in a larger bowl of crushed ice, to which a small quantity of water has been added'.

Victorian cooks dreaded having to make mayonnaise in hot weather, especially when it was thundery. For coloured mayonnaise, traditional additions were lobster coral for red, spinach or parsley for green.

STRAIN A FATTY STOCK THROUGH COLD MUSLIN

A most useful tip for cooks before the days of refrigeration, which works because the fat solidifies on contact with the fine muslin 'sieve'.

If a stock or stew is made with meat and cooked slowly, the fat that runs through the muscle melts into the liquid. Because fat and water do not mix, the fat will, when the dish is left to stand, rise to the top of the pot. If left in a cold place, or chilled, the fat will solidify and can be easily removed. As well as making the dish more palatable, removing the fat is helpful for anyone trying to reduce their calorie intake or to cut down on saturated fats.

Stockfish is an old term for dried cod and other fish, but specifically those that had not been salted.

Good stocks are essential to both gravies (see page 45) and soups. In the opening of his 1854 *Cookery for the People*, Alexis Soyer alerts his fictitious correspondent Eloise to the matter of making stock with these words: 'Please pay attention to the following receipt, for when you are perfect in it, and can make it quick and well, almost every sort of soup can be made from it, and it will be often be referred to in different sauces and dishes.'

Muslin, also called butter muslin or cheesecloth, is useful in the kitchen for fine straining when making jellies, and for wrapping herbs for a bouquet garni and pips when making marmalade. It is still used for lining moulds in cheese making (which by the ambitious can be done at home) and, in days when milk often went sour, was regularly used by thrifty home cooks to strain the curds of their liquid whey to make cheese.

SOFTEN GELATINE IN COLD WATER

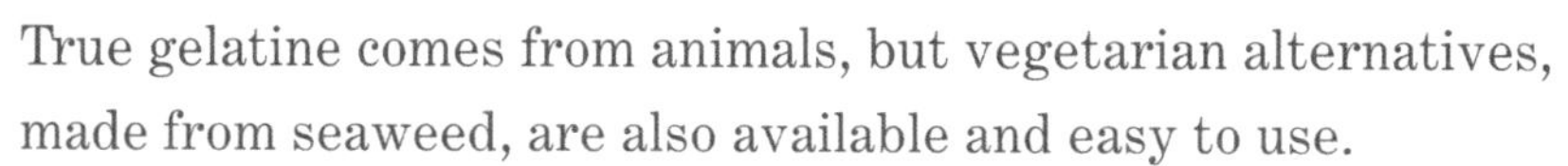

The vital first step in using thin sheets of leaf gelatine, and also for powdered gelatine, to prepare it for use. True gelatine comes from animals, but vegetarian alternatives, made from seaweed, are also available and easy to use.

When soaked in cold water, leaf gelatine swells up. You then squeeze out the excess water with your hands and add it to the liquid in your recipe, heating it gently until it dissolves. For powdered gelatine the recommended method is to sprinkle it on to a little cold water then heat it gently until it dissolves. This has to be carefully done or you risk ending up with a nasty, lumpy mess.

Some cuts of meat, as well as fish such as eels, produce great amounts of gelatine, and when cooked will jellify without any help. Jellied eels are an old Cockney speciality.

Gelatine is a natural product derived from cartilage and other connective tissue in meat and bones, but not hooves and horns. It was once accorded almost magical recuperative powers, but this myth was exploded by the 19th-century German chemist Justus von Liebig, who wrote an exaggerated (and, as it has proved, inaccurate) demolition of its reputation: 'It has now been proved by the most convincing experiments,' he said, 'that gelatine, which by itself is tasteless and when eaten excites nausea, possesses no nutritive value.' In fact gelatine does contain protein, but in small proportion compared with the muscle of meat or fish.

A clear savoury jelly, often used chopped as a garnish or set in a thin layer around a dish, is known as aspic. Cooks would once make it by boiling meat or poultry bones with meat such as shin of beef containing plenty of connective tissue. The liquid, when cooled, produced a jellied stock which, if not firm enough, could be set by adding some extra gelatine.

Vegetarian gelatines from seaweeds come in the form of agar-agar or, for an even better set without the nasty odour that agar-agar can give off during cooking, as carrageen. The red seaweeds from which carrageen is extracted have long been used in Ireland to make a remedy for coughs and colds. They are boiled in milk or water and the strained liquid flavoured with honey and lemon.

DAMPEN A MOULD BEFORE YOU FILL IT

A method advised in old cookbooks for making it easier to unmould a gelatine dessert, but far from infallible. Quickly dipping the set mould into hot water is a better ruse. Whether sweet or savoury, jellied dishes, not least because of their looks, are always crowd pleasers.

Jelly moulds come in all shapes and sizes and are often highly decorative. They can be of metal (copper, tin, aluminium or stainless steel) or of glass, and old ones in good condition are collectors' items. Even older are wooden moulds, used for dishes such as flummeries – jellies made by steeping oatmeal in water overnight and boiling the strained liquid with sugar.

A gilded lèche *or leach, a rosewater jelly decorated with gold leaf, was served at Henry VIII's Garter Feast in 1520. It was related to 'ribband jelly', a dish moulded in multicoloured layers, which was popular from the 17th century.*

For fruit jellies, it was traditional to choose a mould patterned with the fruit in question. *The Concise Household Encyclopedia* of 1933 advises: 'The mould should not be very deep in comparison to the width, or the jelly may break on being turned out. Some moulds,' it continues, 'are made with a deep indentation in the bottom, the corresponding hollow in the jelly then being filled with whipped or clotted cream.'

For a good but not too solid a set, you need to get the proportions just right. For both leaf and powdered gelatine you need about 28g (1oz) to 450ml (1 pint) of liquid, and half this amount to set a thick fruit purée. It is also wise to avoid adding fresh pineapple, kiwi fruit or papaya, all of which contain the enzyme bromelian, which breaks down the gelatine and stops it from setting.

Jello or gelatine shots, known in Britain as vodka jellies, are purported to have been invented in the 1950s by the American mathematician and satirical songwriter Tom Lehrer while he was working for the National Security Agency, as a means of getting around the strict rules forbidding the consumption of alcohol at the base.

SUCCESSFUL JELLY

Some more useful tips:

Spray the inside of the mould, or brush it very lightly with sunflower or some other oil that has no taste.

To suspend fruit or vegetables in a jelly, chill it until it has the consistency of egg whites before you add them.

Never let a gelatine mixture boil or it may lose its gelling properties.

Allow at least two hours for a jelly to set, even in the refrigerator.

Be generous with gelatine in sweet recipes – the more sugar a recipe contains the softer the set will be.

Use gelatine to set a fruit mixture for a cheesecake topping.

Adding alcohol, such as champagne, to a jelly will produce a softer set.

For a 'snow', whisk a jelly when it is half set: it will hold the air bubbles you beat into it, turning pale and opaque with a light texture.

The art of whipping cream is knowing when to stop

Because when overwhipped cream will get too stiff and take on a granular, buttery consistency with liquid weeping from it. While an electric whisk is quicker for whipping than a hand or rotary whisk, it is wise to use it at the lowest possible setting to be sure of a good result.

Cream will not whip successfully unless it contains enough fat – at least 30 and even better 40 per cent – which is why it is impossible to get single or pouring cream to thicken, however much it is beaten. As Harold McGee, renowned expert on culinary chemistry, explains in his book *On Food and Cooking*, 'Whipped cream is an intimate intermingling of liquid and air, with the air divided into tiny bubbles and the cream spread out and immobilized in the microscopically thin bubble walls.'

What happens when you overwhip is that this stable mixture becomes destabilized, so that the fat coagulates, as it does when butter is made. Even well-whipped cream will not stay stable indefinitely without some help, such as the addition of whipped egg white or a little gelatine.

The oldest type of whisk was simply a bunch of twigs tied together. An 18th-century Shaker recipe instructs cooks to: 'Cut a handful of peach twigs which are filled with sap at this season of the year. Clip the ends and bruise them and beat the cake batter with them. This will impart a delicate peach flavor to the cake.' The wire or balloon or egg whisk was an 18th-century invention; the first electric version arrived in kitchens in the early 1900s.

Once whipped, cream can be piped decoratively on to a dessert or folded in. When folded into fruit purée it makes a fruit fool, a dish thought to be named from the French *fouler*, meaning 'to mash'.

Crème chantilly is whipped cream sweetened with sugar and flavoured with vanilla. *Crème fraîche*, however, is a lightly fermented type of cream. Clotted cream, a speciality of England's West Country traditionally eaten with scones and homemade jam, has a buttery crust on top. It is made from cream that is scalded, then cooled, using a method that has remained unchanged for at least 400 years.

Don't boil cream sauces – they will curdle

And be even more careful if there is egg in the sauce, particularly if combined with an acid ingredient like lemon juice or tomatoes. Cheese makers, however, take steps to hasten the reaction that can spell disaster in the kitchen.

When milk curdles it separates into the solid curds and liquid whey eaten by Little Miss Muffet in the nursery rhyme – a process hastened by adding rennet or acid. Curds have long been relished as a nourishing food, notably in Yorkshire where they are used to make curd tarts.

In a perfect sauce, the proteins are changed just enough to thicken the sauce and make it smooth. Curdling happens when you overheat sauces that contain eggs, milk, cream or yoghurt, because the heat makes the proteins they contain solidify or coagulate – a process that cannot be reversed. Before this happens, a mixture may begin to separate, at which point it may be possible to rescue it by cooling it, stirring vigorously, and adding more eggs or cream.

Best of all is to prevent trouble. For egg sauces such as custards, a double boiler or *bain marie*, containing barely simmering water in the lower container, provides a more gentle heat and makes it easier to 'catch' the mixture before it boils. There is a fine line between a perfectly thickened sauce and one that is curdled and spoiled, simply because proteins can coagulate hundreds of times faster at 88°C (190°F) than at 82°C (180°F). When cream or yoghurt are used, especially if there is an acid ingredient such as lemon juice in the sauce, a good trick is to stir in a teaspoon of cornflour before they are added, which effectively binds and stabilizes the mixture.

Melt chocolate over boiling water

The best way to melt chocolate slowly so that it does not overheat, seize up and go grainy, but if mixed with other ingredients such as cream or butter it can be successfully melted in a saucepan over a very low heat. A microwave oven, judiciously used, is also excellent for melting chocolate.

If by accident you overheat chocolate and it seizes you may be able to rescue it by adding a teaspoon of vegetable oil for every 25g (1oz) of chocolate in your pan. Another good tip is to chop the chocolate small before melting it, since this cuts down the amount of heat you need to apply. When melting chocolate in the microwave, begin with a 30-second burst on high, followed by bursts of 5 or 10 seconds until there are no lumps, stirring the mixture between each burst.

Chocolate is made by crushing the seeds (beans) found inside the big, lumpy pods of the cacao tree. When bought in bars it consists of a mixture of cocoa butter and cocoa solids.

This luxurious recipe was written by Edward Kidder, a renowned London pastry maker, in about 1730: 'Take a pt. of cream with a spoonful of scrapt chocolate boyle them well together. Mix with it the yolks of 2 eggs & thicken & mill it on the fier the pour it into your chocolate cups.'

Because the flavour intensifies with the percentage of cocoa solids, the best chocolate to choose for cooking is one containing at least 70 per cent cocoa solids. A good percentage of cocoa butter will help to give a good, smooth melt.

When they introduced chocolate to Europeans, the Aztecs and Mayans claimed it was the food of the gods. But even though he was told that this *xocoatl* was made from god-made beans from the 'Garden of Life', Columbus was not greatly impressed when, in 1502, he tasted his first chocolate drink. And although he took some beans back to Spain nothing was done with them. In 1519, Cortés also encountered the beans but had the foresight to return home with recipes for their use as well as the beans themselves. By the 17th century, chocolate drinking was all the rage and chocoholics abounded. The fact that Maria Theresa, wife of Louis XIV, lost all her teeth was said to be a result of her daily habit of drinking chocolate.

IN PRAISE OF CHOCOLATE

Quotations extolling the virtues of chocolate abound:

'There has always been a suspicion of something dark, powerful, hallucinogenic, and addictive in chocolate.' (Mark Kurlansky)

'Persons who drink chocolate regularly are conspicuous for unfailing health and immunity from a host of minor ailments which mar the enjoyment of life . . .' (Brillat-Savarin)

'What woman has not seen her defenses crumble before a box of chocolates?' (Isabel Allende)

'Only the crumbliest, flakiest chocolate, tastes like chocolate never tasted before.' (Advertisement for Cadbury's Flake, 1976)

'There are four basic food groups: milk chocolate, dark chocolate, white chocolate, and chocolate truffles.' (Anonymous)

'All you need is love. But a little chocolate now and then doesn't hurt'. (Charles M. Schultz)

Smooth icing with a knife dipped in hot water

A handy way for the home cook to finish an icing or frosting, and best done with a wide-bladed smooth-edged palette knife. A hot knife melts the icing a little, making it easy to work. For a more professional finish with royal icing, cake decorators use an icing ruler, held flat and swept back and forth over the surface.

Icing gives a lovely finish to a cake and is easy to make now that icing sugar (also called powdered or confectioner's sugar) is readily available. This type of sugar is relatively recent, having been introduced only towards the end of the 19th century. In his dictionary of the late 1600s, John Knott describes the making of icing. First the sugar had to be 'beaten very fine in a mortar' then sifted, then 'put again in the mortar with four spoonfuls of rose-water, and the whites of two eggs'. As for its use, 'When cakes and tarts come out of the oven,' he instructed, 'dip a feather in your icing and strike over your cakes and tarts and set them in a cool oven to harden.'

'When frosting is too stiff to spread smoothly, thin with a few drops of water. With a pastry bag and a variety of tubes cakes may be ornamented as desired.' (Fannie Merritt Farmer)

Simplest of all is glacé icing, which is just icing sugar and warm water. For royal icing, the sugar is mixed with beaten egg whites and a little glycerine. Fondant icing, which has to be kneaded in the making, calls for icing sugar, liquid glucose or corn syrup and egg whites. Its great advantage is that it can be rolled out before it is put on to a cake. For a sandwich cake, a butter or buttercream icing made with two parts icing sugar to one part butter, and flavoured as you wish, is ideal.

Royal icing is the type used to decorate wedding cakes, which have been iced since the 16th century when refined sugar first became available and affordable. Its pure white colour is a symbol of virginity, while the cake itself is a much older fertility symbol. The 'royal' tag stems from 1840 and the marriage of Queen Victoria to Prince Albert, at which a multilayered cake, iced in white, was eaten. *The Times*, in a detailed account, reported that on the second tier, 'which was supported by two pedestals, a sculpture of "Britannia" gazed upon the royal couple as they exchanged their vows,' and that 'there were several sculpted cupids, including one happily writing the date of the wedding onto a tablet.'

Ice cream must be churned

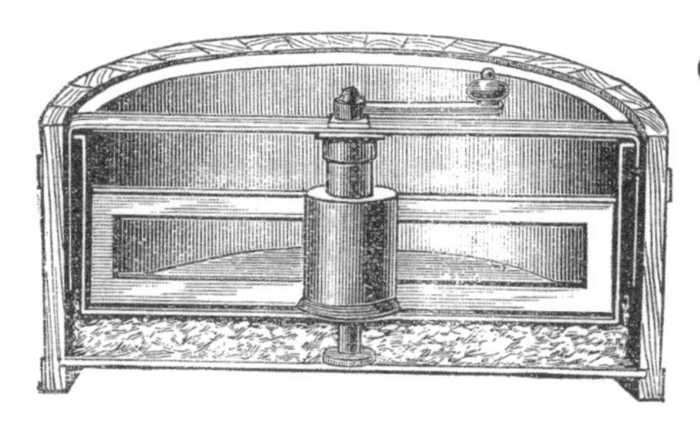

Churning is essential for getting a smooth finish to an ice cream, because it adds the air that helps to break up the ice crystals as they form in the mixture. The first true ice creams, with cream as an ingredient (as opposed to water ices or sorbets), are thought to have been made in Italy in the 17th century.

It is possible to churn ice cream with a whisk, but the modern electric ice cream maker takes all the sweat out of churning. Without an ice cream maker, you will need to beat your mixture two or three times as it freezes, beginning as it starts to become mushy. Less churning or beating is needed for a granita, which is characterized by its large ice crystals.

Although a European invention, ice cream gained huge popularity in America from the mid-18th century. At Mount Vernon in Virginia, George Washington owned a 'Cream Machine for Making Ice' and is recorded as spending much money on ice cream in the summer of 1790. By 1900 an Englishman, Charles Senn, was writing that 'Ices derive their present great popularity from America, where they are consumed during the summer months as well as the winter months in enormous quantities.'

'My advice to you is not to inquire why or whither, but just enjoy your ice-cream while it's on your plate, – that's my philosophy.' (Thornton Wilder)

In the 1890s, Fannie Merritt Farmer was stern in her warning about what she dubbed 'the most popular desserts'. 'Hygienically speaking,' she says, 'they cannot be recommended for the final course of a dinner, as cold mixtures reduce the temperature of the stomach, thus retarding digestion . . . But how cooling, refreshing, and nourishing, when properly taken, and of what inestimable value in the sick room!' She describes in detail how ice cream could be made at home without a freezer using ice and rock salt (to lower the melting point), packed round a metal can whose contents were churned with a crank. 'Snow,' she added, 'may be used instead of ice.'

The first ice cream on a stick was made and sold in 1920 in Youngstown, Ohio, by Harry Burt, the owner of an ice cream parlour. Covered in chocolate and sold from trucks by ice cream vendors, it was called the 'Good Humor Ice Cream Sucker'.

ADD LEMON TO STRAWBERRY JAM TO MAKE IT SET

If you're having real trouble, you also need to add pectin – the natural sticky gel that strawberries lack, which makes jam solidify. Lemon juice helps the setting process by drawing out all the available pectin from the fruit.

The essential process of jam making is simple: boil fruit with an equal weight of sugar until, when a small amount is dabbed on to a cold plate, it sets to a firm consistency. While fruits like plums, currants and gooseberries contain plenty of

The expression 'jam tomorrow', meaning a pleasant thing that remains a dream, comes from Lewis Carroll's *Through the Looking Glass* written in 1871. The White Queen offers Alice, in reward for being her maid, twopence a week and jam every other day. But unfortunately for Alice the deal is 'Jam to-morrow and jam yesterday – but never jam *to-day*.'

natural pectin and jam made with them will set with ease, strawberries and all but the most acid raspberries are notorious for their reluctance to set. Try boiling unpeeled lemon slices and using the resulting liquid (which contains pectin from the fruit pith) or to ensure success use natural pectin, which you can buy ready prepared in powder form or mixed into special preserving sugar.

Jam is a relative newcomer to the kitchen cupboard, being first recorded in the 1730s, some 200 years after solid marmalade (see page 139) and fruit cheeses were originally made. Because it needed so much sugar to ensure a set and good keeping qualities, jam remained a luxury. As Mrs Beeton observed: 'The expense of preserving them [fruits] with sugar is a serious objection; for, except the sugar is used in considerable quantities, the success is very uncertain.'

Jam was strictly rationed in wartime Britain. The weekly allowance per person was just 2oz (55g). Families lucky enough to have relatives living in the USA and Canada were always thrilled when the much-welcomed food parcels contained tins of jam.

A good custard should be perfectly smooth

Whether made with eggs or using custard powder, and whether cooked on top of the stove or baked in the oven, smoothness is indeed an essential of a perfect custard. Custards become lumpy when they cook too quickly or are not stirred enough.

The custard apple is the name given to fruit of the genus Annona, *including the bull's heart and the cherimoya, named for their soft creamy texture and the delicate flavour of their flesh.*

Because it was originally used to bind ingredients in tarts and flans, custard is named from the word *croustade*, a tart with a crust. The custards of the Middle Ages were mixtures of whole eggs and milk that were baked in the oven as it cooled down after bread had been baked. In this way they cooked slowly so that the protein in the egg solidified gradually, leaving a dessert that was creamy and set with no lumps. For a pouring custard, only egg yolks are used, in the proportion of four yolks to 450ml (1 pint) of milk. It is best made in a double saucepan and stirred constantly so that the sauce does not boil, which would scramble the yolks. Sugar and vanilla are classic flavourings, but nutmeg, lemon, chocolate, coffee and caramel are also good.

Custard powder, which thickens milk with a flavoured cornflour mixture, was the invention of the English chemist Alfred Bird in 1837. His stimulus was not the difficulty of making good custard but the fact that his wife, a custard lover, was allergic to eggs. His product immediately became popular, and remains so to this day.

CHAPTER 4

PERFECT VEGETABLES AND FRUIT

'No dinner can be a success unless the vegetables receive proper attention and consideration.' So Mrs Agnes Marshall wisely observed in her *Cookery Book* of 1897, continuing with the equally perceptive statement that 'they should be well dished and present a tempting appearance'. Such sentiments are as valid today as they were in times past, because we know for certain that stale, poorly cooked vegetables not only appear totally unappetizing but are deficient in vitamins and minerals, which are essential to keep both body and mind in tip-top condition. The prudent cook will therefore choose vegetables carefully, opt for those in season and treat them well, knowing that, as a rule, it is best to cook leaf vegetables quickly and root vegetables slowly.

Fruit, too, is best when fresh, especially soft fruits, which may be in peak condition for only a few hours. From oranges and lemons to mangoes and pineapples, the modern cook also has a huge range of more exotic fruit to choose from, which means that selecting the best demands knowledge and experience. In the kitchen, fruits are even more versatile than vegetables, since as well as being served on their own or as an accompaniment to cheese, they marry perfectly with savoury ingredients, and, of course, are the key to superb desserts of all kinds.

If vegetables are cooked a minute too long they lose their beauty and flavour

Particularly if they are green vegetables such as cabbage, which can turn from being deliciously crunchy to a soggy mass in a matter of seconds. For root vegetables, which need longer cooking, timing is less of an issue.

To prevent the smell of boiling vegetables permeating the house, an old tip was to put a piece of bread wrapped in muslin into the pan. A little vinegar 'kept boiling on the stove while onions or cabbage are being cooked' was also recommended, although one would imagine this would make the smell worse rather than better.

In former times vegetables were often cooked for longer than is advised today, and it was the habit to add soda to the water to help preserve their colour. Mrs Beeton, however, was precise about the need to avoid overcooking cabbage. Having trimmed and cut the cabbage into quarters, she instructed the cook to '. . . put them into *plenty* of *fast-boiling* water, to which have been added salt and soda . . . Stir them down once or twice in the water, keep the pan uncovered, and let them boil quickly until tender. The instant they are done, take them up into a colander, place a plate over them, let them drain thoroughly, dish and serve.'

Cooks of old also recommended starting root vegetables off in cold water but plunging green vegetables (or those like cauliflower that grow above ground) into boiling water. They would have known that fast cooking produces the best results because 'slow boiling spoils the colour of all green vegetables', but not that it is also the best way of preserving the vitamins and minerals they contain.

The English, it seems for good reason, acquired a reputation for producing poorly cooked, under-seasoned vegetables and for serving them as part of the main course – as in 'meat and two veg'. This was in contrast to the French, who habitually served beautifully cooked vegetables as a separate dish at the end of a dinner.

COOKS' TIPS

More tried and trusted guidelines for cooking vegetables:

Cook stem vegetables quickly, root vegetables slowly.

Plunge vegetables into boiling water for maximum retention of their vitamin content.

All kinds of root vegetables can be roasted – as can vegetable fruits such as peppers, courgettes (zucchini) and aubergines (egg plant).

Boiled vegetables always need to be well drained.

Any vegetable will make a nourishing soup.

Washed spinach needs no water added. Just shake the pan over the heat until the leaves wilt.

Keep in the goodness by steaming or grilling vegetables rather than boiling them.

Vegetables need to sweat – that is, to be browned and softened before being added to a soup or casserole.

Know your onions

Not originally an instruction to the cook, but still worth taking literally, since there are so many different kinds of onions, all of which add incomparable flavour to savoury dishes. The saying may refer to the famous lexicographer, C. T. Onions, or come from 'onion rings' – Cockney rhyming slang for 'things'.

An onion or shallot kept in the pocket will ward off illness.

Large white onions are the type most used in cooking and were grown in ancient Egypt from at least 3200 BC. Best for flavour and mildness are varieties of Spanish and Egyptian onions. Milder yet are red onions, which will not overpower a dish even when eaten raw. Spring or green onions, also called scallions, are a type of onion bred to be eaten when immature. Some sorts, including oriental and bunching onions, grow, as their name suggests, in small clumps. Small silverskin onions are available for pickling (see page 198), while for a mild, subtle flavour shallots are the cook's best choice.

According to Alexandre Dumas' *Grand Dictionnaire de Cuisine*, published in 1873, an enterprising Frenchman from Roscoff in Brittany (from where onions were regularly exported to England) persuaded Londoners to buy his onions by erecting a placard in a busy market announcing: 'The English onion is not good.' Underneath, he placed a little barrow full of French ones, which sold out within the day. Until the 1990s French onion sellers from Brittany regularly cycled around English towns peddling their wares.

A girl would put an onion under her pillow to ensure that she would dream of the man she was going to marry.

Of all the dishes that the French make with onions, the highlights include French onion soup and Alsatian onion tart. In British cuisine, onion sauce is a classic accompaniment to roast lamb, and sage and onion stuffing is served with roast pork, duck or goose.

Boil beetroots in their skins

For the simple reason that this stops them 'bleeding' into the cooking water, and keeps the deep red colour contained inside the root. When washing raw beetroots, remember to avoid cutting off the long tapering root.

Beetroot takes an age to boil and, as Fannie Merritt Farmer rightly commented, 'Old beets will never be tender, however long they may be cooked.' In English cuisine, cooked beetroots have a poor reputation as intrusive salad vegetables that colour everything they touch, or as acid pickles, but a classic beetroot soup or borscht is hard to beat. Miss Farmer gives a recipe for sugared beets, which are reheated, after cooking, with butter, sugar and salt, rather like glazed carrots. Small, young beetroots are delicious cooked whole and served with a mustard sauce as a starter. Or try grating them raw and tossing them in a dressing of lemon juice, crème fraîche and plenty of dill, salt and freshly ground black pepper.

In Germany the yellow beet is known as the *Mangelwurzel*, literally 'root for time of need' (*Mangel* means 'scarcity') because it was eaten when no other food was available. The name is a punning corruption of *Mangoldwurzel*, which simply means 'beet root'.

The Greeks were probably the first to cultivate beetroot, though the roots were almost certainly yellow, not red, and were long and thin like parsnips in shape. Swollen round roots were first recorded in the 1550s, and red or Roman beets were not eaten in Britain until the 17th century. Before this, only the yellow sorts were grown, and although these subsequently went out of general cultivation for centuries, seeds of such varieties as 'Burpees Golden' are now available once more.

Scrape carrots – don't peel them

Fine advice for small, young carrots, but for old ones it may be necessary to take off the bitter, outer layer of these tasty, sweet roots. Such preparation also helps stop carrots from discolouring during cooking.

In the kitchen, carrots have a long tradition. The Babylonians, Greeks and Romans probably made use of the aromatic tops and seeds of small wild carrots with bitter-tasting roots. By the Middle Ages carrots of a deep purple-red colour were being enjoyed in Europe, often as an affordable sweetener in cakes and puddings, mimicking their traditional role in Asian cookery as ingredients for jams and preserves. Not until the 17th century were the orange carrots we know today bred for eating.

Carrots reached England as a rare delicacy in the reign of Elizabeth I. One story tells of a deputation to court presenting her with a tub of butter and a wreath of tender carrots emblazoned with diamonds. She is said to have removed the diamonds and sent the carrots and butter to the kitchen from where they returned as the classic side dish of buttered carrots.

During World War II carrots were widely used as a sweet ingredient in carrot jams, cakes and puddings. The carrot cake now served with a cream cheese topping came into vogue in the USA in the 1960s and has been a firm favourite ever since.

It is true that carrots can make you see better in the dark. They are packed with vitamin A, which combines chemically with a protein at the back of the eye to form rhodopsin, the substance essential for night vision.

In the savoury range, carrots are ideal ingredients for soups and stews. The classic carrot soup *potage Crécy* is named for the region in France where they are reputed to have the best flavour. It was once customary for loyal Britons to eat this dish each year on 26 August to celebrate the anniversary of the English victory over the French at Crécy in 1346.

Boiled beef and carrots – a quintessentially English combination beloved of London Cockneys – is celebrated in a music hall song of 1909 written by Charles Collins and Fred Murray and made famous by Harry Champion.

Boiled beef and carrots,
Boiled beef and carrots,
That's the stuff for your Derby Kell,
Makes you fit and keeps you well.
Don't live like vegetarians
On the stuff they give to parrots,
From Morn til' night, blow out your kite
On boiled beef and carrots.

('Derby Kell' is cockney rhyming slang: Derby Kelly – belly; 'kite' is slang for the stomach or the whole body.)

Crush garlic, don't chop it

Chopping garlic – and pressing it through a metal crusher even more so – is the surest way to release the acrid chemicals it contains. A decisive bash with a wooden rolling pin or a swift crush beneath the flat of a knife blade is the best way to avoid the problem.

What happens when garlic is cut is that the enzyme allinase contained in its cells comes in contact and combines with a chemical called alliin to make allicin, one of the substances that makes garlic smell. This quickly breaks down – and more quickly still when the cells are chopped through with a knife – into the really acrid smelling diallyl disulphide, the unmistakable garlic odour.

Avoiding garlic's acridity is especially important if it is to be used raw. For a fine dice, crush it first then chop it as quickly as you can. All garlic will,

In Mediterranean cooking, garlic is the essential ingredient of aïoli, a mayonnaise eaten with cold meat and fish. In *aïoli garni* it is served with a mixture of hot, boiled ingredients including, by tradition, cod, snails, squid, fennel, onions and potatoes.

however, mellow on cooking. Roast garlic has a wonderfully mild flavour. Cut the top off whole heads, drizzle them with olive oil and add a sprinkling of sea salt crystals; bake them at 200°C/400°F/ Gas 6 for 45–60 minutes.

Garlic was once dubbed 'poor man's treacle' for its health-giving properties. Modern medicine confirms that it helps to lower blood pressure and blood cholesterol, kills bacteria and viruses and acts as a nasal decongestant. It may even help to prevent cancer. However, Nicholas Culpeper advised strongly against eating too much garlic because it could create 'strange visions in the head'.

Green peas are best when young

There is nothing quite like the taste of fresh young green peas, eaten raw straight from the pod, and for cooking these are the best of all. By country tradition, a lucky pod containing nine peas was hung over the door by a young girl. The first man to enter beneath it was the one she would marry.

After the pea harvest, the pods were traditionally made into peascod soup, but the custom has died out now that so much of the crop is grown for freezing.

In Europe, peas have been enjoyed since at least 3000 BC and were well known to the Greeks and Romans, but in their fully mature and dried form. By the Middle Ages, dried peas were the staple food of the poor and were made into filling, protein-rich dishes such as pease pudding, which was eaten with bacon or other meat when available.

Garden peas were bred in the 16th century and by the end of the 1600s eating immature green peas was all the rage, especially in France. Madame de Maintenon, a member of the court of Louis XIV, wrote that 'There are ladies who, even after having supped with the King, go home and there eat a dish of green peas before going to bed. It is both a fashion and a madness.' Petits pois were originally peas eaten very young and small, but varieties are now bred to mature at a miniature size. A dish of 'peas cooked in the French style' describes peas stewed with butter, spring onions (scallions) and shredded lettuce and flavoured with salt and sugar.

Peas were one of the first vegetables to be frozen by Clarence Birdseye. He discovered the possibilities of deep freezing while working in Labrador from 1912–15, when during fishing expeditions his catch froze instantly at -40°C/F.

PEAS OF MANY SORTS

Peas come in a variety of forms. Although all are legumes, not all are true peas:

Mangetouts – a catch-all term for peas bred to be eaten whole. The name means literally 'eat all'.

Pigeon peas – tropical peas mostly grown in India where, dried, they are called dal or dhal and used for the curried dish of the same name.

Marrowfat peas – large, fat peas mostly grown for canning; they are also made into mushy peas, served with fish and chips.

Asparagus peas – a type of mangetout with winged pods best eaten when only about 25mm (1in) long. They are the young fruits of a type of vetch.

Chickpeas – relations of the pea grown since ancient times and said to be named for the Roman orator Cicero, who had an ancestor with a wart on his face shaped like a dried chickpea. The essential ingredient of hummus.

The tough rind of a cucumber is best avoided

A sentiment expressed by Eliza Acton and certainly true of ridge and other outdoor cucumbers, which, unlike hothouse varieties, have thick, indigestible skins. As well as dressed cucumbers for salads, the Acton repertoire included many cooked cucumber dishes.

In additional to peeling, Miss Acton recommended that cucumbers be disgorged like aubergines with 'a little fine salt' before being used, then coated with 'the purest salad oil' and 'chili vinegar'. Her Mandrang, a recipe from the West Indies for serving 'with any kind of roast meat', mixed chopped cucumber and onion, lemon juice, salt, cayenne pepper and one or two glasses of Madeira or dry white wine. Cooked cucumbers, to serve as a side dish, were fried in butter and served in a stock thickened with egg yolks and flavoured with parsley, salt and pepper. Or they were peeled and sliced, dusted with flour and fried as an accompaniment to 'common hashes and minces'.

Mrs Beeton was careful to warn her readers of the possible disadvantages of eating cucumbers. 'Generally speaking,' she said, 'delicate stomachs should avoid this plant, for it is cold and indigestible.' The 17th-century herbalist Nicholas Culpeper took a somewhat opposite view, proclaiming them 'excellently good for a hot stomach, and hot liver . . .' He also recommended the seeds for urinary and bladder health, and the juice for cleansing the skin and for treating 'sun-burning and freckles'.

The Armenian cucumber or snake melon is, as its name suggests, not a true cucumber but a type of melon. From its size it is sometimes called the yard-long cucumber. Its flesh is sweet, not bitter, and the pale yellow skin is thin and edible.

Wipe, don't wash mushrooms

The theory behind this age-old advice is that washing mushrooms makes them soggy, but since these vegetables are already 90 per cent water, a little more is not likely to make much difference.

Preparation method, therefore, is the cook's prerogative, though the tenacity with which pieces of dirt cling to the cups often makes washing the only practical cleaning method. Peeling today's cultivated mushrooms is almost always unnecessary, but may improve large field mushrooms gathered from the wild. For fine dishes the stalks of mushrooms are best removed, and the frugal cook will keep them for flavouring stocks or stews.

Shirley Conran introduced her 1975 bestseller *Superwoman* with the motto: 'Life is too short to stuff a mushroom.'

Most mushrooms we cook and eat today are cultivated – and have been since the 17th century, when the French discovered how to 'sow' the underground filaments or mycelia, from which the mushrooms grow, in beds of asses' dung. Mushrooms were traditionally stewed with butter and served under roast poultry or, in the 19th century, presented stuffed as an entrée. As a savoury – a dish served at the end of an English dinner during the 19th and early 20th centuries – mushrooms on toast was a popular choice.

Mushrooms have not always been trusted. John Gerard, in his *Herbal* of 1633, said 'Most of them do suffocate and strangle the eater,' while Nicholas Culpeper believed that 'Inwardly they are unwholesome, and unfit for the strongest constitutions.'

Irish folklore maintains that if you see a button mushroom you should pluck it, as it will not grow any more once it has been looked at.

Truffles are the aristocrats of mushrooms

They are, on account of their unique earthy but delicate aroma and flavour – and the huge prices that even single truffles command. Just a fine shaving of truffle will transform a simple dish such as scrambled eggs: a combination said to be a marriage made in heaven.

'The truffle is not an outright aphrodisiac, but it may in certain circumstances make women more affectionate and men more amiable.' (Brillat-Savarin)

Truffles come in two forms, white and black, and in several varieties. Best known and appreciated are white or Alba truffles (*Tuber magnatum pico*), which grow only in the Piedmont area of northern Italy, and the more common black truffles, including the gnarled black Périgord truffles (*T. melanosporum*) which, despite their name, are also found in Provence. Truffle hunters – who often go out at night – use dogs and pigs to help locate their treasure. One tell-tale sign of their location is said to be flies hovering over a spot on the ground.

Scientists analysing the aroma of black truffles have identified more than 100 different scents, described as everything from earthy, nutty and grassy to citrus, vanilla and rose petal. The fresher the truffle the greater the complexity of its aromas. White truffles, by contrast, have a more intense musky and sulphurous odour, with beefy and umami (soy-type) elements.

If you are lucky enough to acquire a truffle of either sort, make the most of it by cutting it as finely as possible with a truffle slice and shaving it over hot, rather than cold food, so that its aromas can permeate as fully as possible. A sauce so enriched will be totally transformed. And use it at once, for the perfect aroma of a fresh truffle quickly fades. Top chefs wrap their truffles in foil and keep them in the refrigerator unwashed or clean them and pack them in jars of Armagnac.

Are they worth more than diamonds? In the 19th century black truffles were so common that in France they were eaten as a vegetable like any other. Today, a measure of truffle value and scarcity is that in December 2007 a single white truffle weighing 1.5kg (3.3lb) sold for £165,000 ($330,000).

Store celery in a jug of water

A good way of preventing a head of celery from becoming limp and flabby, even if it is kept in the refrigerator. It is rumoured that Madame de Pompadour invented a celery soup to inflame the desires of Louis XV, so validating its aphrodisiac qualities.

Bred from a wild plant called smallage, celery was first used in the kitchen as a flavouring rather than a vegetable. In the *Odyssey* Homer calls it *selinon* and the Greeks made it into garlands for funerals. As milder forms were bred from the 17th century onwards, celery cemented its place as a salad ingredient. Writing in this period the naturalist John Ray said of it: 'Smallage transferred to culture becomes milder and less ungrateful, whence in Italy and France the leaves and stalks are esteemed as delicacies, eaten with oil and pepper.'

In the 18th and early 19th centuries, celery dipped in egg and breadcrumbs and fried featured in many recipes, some of which recommend parboiling the celery first to remove any bitterness. Celery sauce – a sieved

For times when fresh celery was not available, *Enquire Within* recommended making essence of celery of which 'a few drops will flavour a pint of soup or broth equal to a head of celery'. The method was to soak for a fortnight 'half an ounce of the seeds of celery in a quarter pint of brandy'.

mixture of cooked celery and onion in a béchamel sauce was recommended as an accompaniment to poultry or game. Celery hearts braised with onions and carrots and a good stock are soft and packed with flavour.

With onions and bell peppers, celery is one of the 'holy trinity' of vegetables essential to the Creole and Cajun cuisines of Lousiana. In the East, it has a similar role but a different variety, namely Chinese celery, a smaller version of the western type, with thinner, crisp, hollow stems that come in dark green or white. This is a staple in the making of Asian soups, stir fries and stews.

Roughen up your roast potatoes

. . . after you have peeled and parboiled them. Roughening up the surface with a fork, or by shaking them hard in a colander, makes them absorb fat better. For roasting, many cooks swear that goose fat gives the most splendidly crisp results.

The potato is said to have become a staple of the English kitchen because of the poor quality of the country's bread and of other vegetables, so giving it 'importance beyond its merit'.

To accompany a Sunday roast joint or chicken, roast potatoes are a must. It is possible to roast new potatoes, but main crop or 'old' potatoes are the best choice by far. Varieties to look for are 'Desirée', 'King Edward', 'Cara', 'Maris Piper' and 'Picasso'. The traditional way of cooking them is in the same pan as the meat, or in dripping, seasoned with salt and pepper, but the modern cook might choose to cook them separately. In a hot oven, which is essential for a crispy exterior, they will need to cook for about an hour.

Goose fat is brilliant for roast potatoes, making them crunchy without being greasy. Technically, the reason is that goose fat will heat to a high temperature before it reaches its 'burn point'. Also goose fat has a deep flavour imparted by the presence of 'umami', the savoury taste that gives foods such as soya sauce their distinctive taste. As well as potatoes the fat is great for roasting all root vegetables (and used in place of lard it will make exceptional pastry for a savoury pie). Failing goose fat, olive oil is an excellent choice.

Rubbing goose fat all over the skin – and especially on the chest – was an old way of keeping out the cold.

Fresh asparagus needs little dressing

A saying that pays tribute to the heavenly taste of fresh spears. Butter or good extra virgin olive oil – or perhaps a vinaigrette – is all it needs, or a subtle hollandaise.

For cooking asparagus, the trick is to boil the stems and steam the tips, so that both are ready at the same time. A tall pan is ideal for the purpose, and tying the asparagus in bunches will help to keep it in place as it cooks. It can also be brushed with olive oil and grilled or roasted.

Hollandaise, a sauce thought to be derived from one brought to France by the Huguenots, marries perfectly with asparagus. Writing

As *Kettner's Book of the Table* aptly says: 'There is no cooked vegetable which raises expectation and lures the fancy so much as asparagus.'

in his cookbook *Le cuisinier françois* in 1651 François Pierre de la Varenne gives this recipe for 'asparagus in fragrant sauce': 'Choose the largest [asparagus], scrape the bottoms and wash, then cook in water, salt well, and don't let them cook too much. When cooked, put them to drain, make a sauce with good fresh butter, a little vinegar, salt, and nutmeg, and an egg yolk to bind the sauce; take care that it doesn't curdle; and serve the asparagus garnished as you like.'

As for the proper way to eat asparagus, the American guru Emily Post recommends in *Etiquette* (1960) that although 'by reputation this is a finger food . . . the ungraceful appearance of a bent stalk of asparagus falling limply into someone's mouth and the fact that moisture is also likely to drip from the end have been the reasons that most fastidious people invariably eat it – at least in part – with the fork.'

Turnips and swedes need the same treatment

Advice that is true for large, mature vegetables, but small young turnips can be treated very differently, making them much more versatile. The swede is also called the rutabaga.

Boiled turnips were a winter staple in ancient times, originally as the swollen, edible roots of wild plants, and were an important element in the Roman diet, but swedes are a more recent addition to the menu, arriving only in the 17th century. And while swedes can come in a variety of colours, the rutabaga, from the Swedish *rotabagge*, meaning 'root bag' always has a yellow flesh. (The name comes from its bulbous shape.)

When a Scots host offers you haggis with 'neeps' your vegetable will be mashed swede. The reason is that the word comes from *Brassica napus*, the scientific name for swede, which the Scots prefer.

Turnips have a stronger flavour than swedes, which is why they are better eaten when young. They make a perfect addition to a *navarin du printemps* – a lamb casserole with spring vegetables – and combine excellently with rich poultry in *caneton aux navets*, in which glazed turnips are added to a dish of braised duckling. Simply glazed, and with chopped fresh herbs added, they are a good side dish. Adding sugar in this way helps to neutralize the bitterness of the flesh; many old recipe books suggest adding sugar to the water in which old turnips are boiled. Mashing both turnips and swedes with butter, pepper and nutmeg also greatly improves their flavour.

There is a salad for every season

Salad can be eaten on every day of the year and is even more enjoyable when made with in-season vegetables – lettuce, tomatoes and cucumber in summer; cabbage, chicory and celery in winter. But almost any ingredients, raw or cooked, can be used in a salad, depending on what takes your fancy.

Vegetables were certainly eaten raw, dressed with salt or oil and vinegar, long before the 14th century when the words 'sallet' and 'salad', from the Latin *sal* (meaning 'salt') came into use. A recipe of the period, advising that everything be 'plucked small', includes leeks, spring onions and watercress as well as fresh mint, sage, parsley, fennel, rosemary and rue. From medieval times fruit – and

The Romans cultivated rocket (arugula), for its spicy seeds as well as for its leaves; the 'wild' type, whose peppery flavour has hints of horseradish, is best of all.

edible flowers – have been included in the list of salad ingredients. By the 17th century, the age of the 'grand sallet', an even greater range of ingredients was used. The most elaborate salads could include cold chicken combined with, among other things, capers, olives, samphire, pickled mushrooms, potatoes, oranges and currants. From this time on, salads were regularly set in aspic and served in elaborately moulded shapes.

Modern salads reflect the wide range of leafy vegetables cultivated for eating raw – including chicory, endive (frisée), beet leaves, baby spinach, rocket and mizuna.

In times when fresh green vegetables were hard to come by in winter the frugal cook would keep any cold cooked vegetables and use them in salad. Beetroot, turnips, carrots and cauliflower were all included, mixed with economical ingredients such as hard-boiled eggs, and dressed with capers and mayonnaise.

SALADS GALORE

Some famous salads from around the world:

Russian salad – probably invented by Lucien Olivier, French owner and chef of the Hermitage restaurant in Moscow in the 1860s. A salad of potatoes with chicken (originally game) with green peas and diced carrots bound with mayonnaise.

Salade niçoise – a salad incorporating ingredients favoured by the chefs of Nice, including tomatoes, anchovies, black olives, capers, garlic and lemon juice. French beans may also be added.

Waldorf salad – epicure Oscar Michel Tschirky, maître d'hotel at New York's Waldorf Hotel, is usually credited with inventing this salad in 1893. The original dish comprised only apples, celery and mayonnaise. Walnuts were a 1920s addition.

Caesar salad – believed to be named for the restaurateur Caesar Cardini, who invented it for guests in Tijuana, Mexico, in 1924 from what was left over in the kitchen – romaine lettuce, garlic, croutons, Parmesan cheese, boiled eggs, olive oil and Worcestershire sauce.

Coleslaw – a salad of cabbage and carrots named in the USA in the late 19th century from the Dutch *koolsla*, an abbreviation of *koolsalade*, or cabbage salad.

Insalata tricolore – an Italian salad of mozzarella (white), tomatoes (red) and basil (green), representing the colours of the Italian flag. Avocado may also constitute the green element. When made with basil it is also called *insalata caprese* (salad in the style of Capri).

Tear lettuce, don't chop it

Chopping lettuce, believe many cooks, imparts an undesirable 'flavour of the knife', and quickly makes salads go limp and brown. But it is often the only way to deal satisfactorily with the ubiquitous 'Icebergs' eaten by the billion each year.

In the 17th century French cooks candied lettuce hearts with sugar to make the confection known as *gorge d'ange* or angel's throat.

Tearing lettuce is said to damage it less because it divides the leaf along the natural boundaries between the cells. In fact, left only to the air, lettuce leaves will not (unlike basil leaves) brown quickly, however they are prepared, but the test comes when you add the dressing. An oily dressing will stick to the leaf and ooze into any breaks in its outer layer or cuticle, creating a browning reaction. Vinegar, by contrast (as with lemon juice on avocado) will stop or effectively delay the same chemical effect.

Lettuce (*Lactuca sativa*), is named for the milky sap that is exuded from its stems and leaves. In ancient times this was associated with fertility, and the Egyptian god Min possessed a sacred bull that was fed on lettuce to maximize its potency. In the Middle Ages, however, eating lettuce was widely thought to cause sterility.

The Greek physician Hippocrates extolled the healing virtues of lettuce (though he may have been referring to wild 'loose' lettuce, *L. serriola*, which makes no heads), but it was not widely cultivated in Europe until the Roman period. In the early days of the Roman Empire, lettuce salad was served at the end of a meal to help induce sleep. Later it became favoured as an appetizer, to stimulate the palate.

The sedative qualities of lettuce are well known and quoted by many authors, including Beatrix Potter in the opening to her much-loved children's book *The Tale of the Flopsy Bunnies*: 'It is said that the effect of eating too much lettuce is "soporific". *I* have never felt sleepy after eating lettuces; but then *I* am not a rabbit.'

A SALAD DRESSING REQUIRES A SPENDTHRIFT FOR OIL, A JUDGE FOR SALT, A MISER FOR VINEGAR AND A MADMAN TO MIX THEM

An old Spanish saying that perfectly describes the ingredients of a good salad dressing, the fact that they need vigorous mixing to blend them, the necessity of judicious seasoning and the fact that too much dressing will make a salad greasy and unappetizing.

A great salad dressing needs a good olive oil (such as an Italian one from Lucca) as the proverb implies, although many cooks prefer to use oil and vinegar in equal quantities. For superior flavour an extra virgin olive oil is the best choice. The mixing demanded results from the fact that oil and vinegar do not physically coalesce. When they are shaken together the oil divides into tiny droplets suspended in the vinegar, but the two will separate again if the dressing is left to stand.

A poem about potato salad by the Victorian scholar Sydney Smith contains pertinent lines on the making of salad dressing:

Of mordant mustard, add a single spoon,
Distrust the condiment that bites too soon;
But deem it not, thou man of herbs, a fault,
To add a double quantity of salt;
Three times the spoon with oil of Lucca crown,
And once with vinegar, procured from town . . .

As with the oil, high quality red or white wine vinegar is a requisite for a good dressing. The 21st-century vogue is for balsamic vinegar, made in Modena in Italy from the long fermentation and acidification of a special variety of grapes, but it needs to be used sparingly or it will overwhelm the dish. Finally, according to Fannie Merritt Farmer, 'Salads made of greens should always be served crisp and cold.'

Watercress is the poor man's bread

Or so it was called in cash-strapped families when it was eaten alone and not in a sandwich, as was the English breakfast custom. When sold in Victorian street markets such as London's Covent Garden it was made into bunches and consumed from the hand like an ice cream cone.

Peppery watercress is a perfect ingredient for a salad or soup, and weight for weight it contains more vitamin C than an orange, more calcium than milk and more iron than spinach. Its heat comes from the mustard oils it contains, which are released when the leaves are chewed; this pungency led to its old name of 'nose twister'. When watercress is cooked, these oils can quickly lose their flavour, which is why it is best to add the leaves to a soup or hot sauce at the last minute so they are just gently wilted.

Watercress has been credited with many healing powers. The herbalist John Gerard rightly believed that it could help prevent scurvy, while Nicholas Culpeper claimed, 'Watercress potage is a good remedy to cleanse the blood in spring and consume the gross humours winter hath left behind.' For the Anglo-Saxons watercress was a salad eaten to prevent baldness.

Although watercress grows wild it is unwise to pick and eat it from country streams, as there is a danger of it being contaminated with the eggs of the liver fluke, a virulent parasite. For the same reason, a supply of pure spring water is an essential element of watercress cultivation.

In the 16th century commercial watercress cultivation was first attempted by Nicholas Meissner at Erfurt in Germany, where it was witnessed by an officer in Napoleon's army and subsequently introduced to France. Watercress became a must at nearly every meal, and the emperor himself was said to be a huge enthusiast.

PEARS ARE PERFECT FOR ONE DAY ONLY

A saying acknowledging the fact that pears can be reluctant to ripen and that once ripe they quickly lose their firmness and become 'sleepy'. The best pears have flesh that is soft and juicy, without a markedly stony texture.

Smell, as well as touch, is the sense you need to test a pear for ripeness. It should have a sweet aroma with no hint of acidity. Even if it is impossible to catch a pear exactly on the right day, cooking pears that are a little underripe are excellent poached or stewed. Since medieval times, pears have been served in a wine-based syrup flavoured with cinnamon and ginger.

The pear (*Pyrus* spp.) originated, with the apple, in the Caucasus and was long considered the superior fruit, especially by the Greeks and Romans. Pears have subsequently been bred to produce the thousand and more varieties now known. In England, the Warden pear, bred by Cistercian monks in Berkshire in medieval times, and also known as the Shakespeare, was a staple for cooking until the plethora of breeding in the 16th and 17th centuries that resulted in sweeter, less gritty, eaters.

Pears were first grown in America after the Massachusetts Company imported seeds from England in 1629. The Williams pear, first grown in Berkshire in 1770 by John Stair, a schoolmaster, is known in America as the Bartlett after Enoch Bartlett, who took it there in the following century. The Seckel, a spicy American pear, is said to have been discovered by a trapper in 1765 on a piece of land he had purchased.

PEARS AND NAMES

Pears and pear dishes have many associations:

Poires Belle-Hélène – poached pears with vanilla ice cream, chocolate and crystallized violets, named from Offenbach's 1864 operetta about Helen of Troy.

Pears Bristol – poached pears mixed with oranges and an orange syrup and topped with pieces of caramel. Named for the city port.

Poires Brillat-Savarin – pears poached in rum and used to fill Genoese sponge, baked and served covered with an apricot pulp. Named for the French gourmet.

Pear charlotte – made in the same way as apple charlotte, with bread, sugar and melted butter, and like it named for George III's queen.

All kinds of apples will make a fine tart

True, as long as you're sure what kind of tart – or other dessert – you wish to make. Most important from the cook's point of view is to know whether or not the apple flesh will keep its shape when cooked. In praise of apples, the epicure Edward Bunyard said: 'Is there any other edible which is at once an insurance, a pleasure and an economy?'

Apples are one of the cook's most versatile ingredients, and even apple tarts come in different forms. The simplest is a classic French *tarte aux pommes*, which consists of a pastry shell filled with eating apples cut into fine slices and arranged cartwheel fashion. After baking it is brushed with a glaze of apricot jam. More complex is a tart filled first with stewed cooking apples, then topped with eating apple slices. A Messina apple tart has raisins added to sliced eating apples and is topped with a mixture of sugar and cinnamon.

A perfect cooking apple, such as the Bramley (correctly, 'Bramley's Seedling') has flesh that is firm when raw but soft and of even consistency when it 'falls' into a pulp. 'Grenadier' is another good variety for cooking. As well as needing to be sweetened with sugar, stewed apples are enormously improved by the addition of a knob of butter and, for flavour, a couple of cloves or a little cinnamon. Sour green apples used for cooking were once commonly known as codlings, possibly from the old word 'coddle' for stewing, simmering or gentle boiling.

For making baked apples and preparing apple rings an apple corer is a handy tool whose design has remained essentially unchanged since the 19th century.

The best dessert apples, by contrast, keep their shape well in a tart or flan. Good old-fashioned choices include 'Cox's Orange Pippin', 'Worcester Permain', which has a pretty red colour, a green 'Granny Smith' or an orange 'Egremont Russet'.

MORE APPLE CLASSICS

Apple charlotte – alternate layers of cooking apples, sugar and breadcrumbs or thin slices of stale bread, flavoured with lemon zest. The whole is topped with melted butter before being baked in the oven. The dish is said to be named for Queen Charlotte, wife of George III, but the word charlotte is also probably a corruption of the Old English word *charlyt*, meaning a 'dish of custard'.

Apple fritters – dessert apple rings, peeled, dipped in fritter batter and deep fried then served dusted with caster sugar.

Baked apples – cooking apples cored and filled with sugar and raisins or sultanas mixed with cinnamon, and baked in a dish with a few spoonfuls of water added. Butter can also be added and mincemeat makes an excellent alternative filling.

Apple dumplings – cooking apples cored and with sugar placed in the centre, wrapped in suet pastry and baked in the oven.

Apple turnovers – apples stewed with sugar, butter and cloves then enclosed in pastry and baked.

Apple crumble – cooking apples (and, in autumn even better with blackberries added), sweetened with sugar and topped with a crumble mixture of butter, flour and demerara sugar. Cinnamon and flaked almonds can also be added to the topping for extra flavour.

A ripe fig should be consumed without delay

A perfect fresh fig is a treat for those partial to these sweet, fleshy delicacies. And it was probably the fig tree, not the apple tree, that bore the fruit that tempted Adam and Eve in the Garden of Eden.

The Athenian dramatist Aristophanes declared that 'nothing is sweeter than figs'.

From ancient times the fig has been grown widely throughout Asia, the Near East and the Mediterranean. One of its great advantages was that the fruit kept well when dried, so was a useful addition to the winter diet. The Egyptians considered figs so valuable that they were placed for sustenance, and for their mildly laxative health-giving properties, in the tombs of the dead for use in the afterlife. From their shape and their plethora of pips, figs are also renowned as aphrodisiacs.

In the British climate, where fig trees flourish but the fruit ripens with reluctance, it became customary to poach green figs very gently for two or three hours in a sugar syrup with lemon rind added for flavour. They were then served cold as a fig compote.

The fig roll, a pastry confection filled with fig jam, was created in 1891 by Charles M. Roser of the Kennedy Biscuit Company in Massachusetts. It was originally called the Newton after the nearby city; the name was changed to Fig Newton in 1898.

Figgy pudding, which features in the song 'We Wish You a Merry Christmas', is a seasonal dish dating from the 17th century,

which developed from frumenty, the spiced porridge of the medieval festive table. The pudding, a mixture of figs, breadcrumbs, suet, sugar, eggs and nutmeg boiled in a cloth, was also made in Lent, both as a Mothering Sunday delicacy and as a dish to celebrate Palm or so-called Fig Sunday. The latter was a custom based on the Biblical account of the withering of the fig tree following the triumphal entry of Jesus into Jerusalem.

GOOSEBERRIES NEED TO BE TOPPED AND TAILED

Snipping off both ends of gooseberries to leave a smooth fruit is a therapeutic job ideally done outside on a sunny day. The 'tail' is the stalk, the 'top' the remnants of the flower. Alternative names for the fruit are the carberry, wineberry and feaberry or feabes.

The tartness of unsweetened gooseberry sauce makes it a perfect foil for the fattiness of goose, duck or mackerel. But after topping and tailing, gooseberries are arguably best made into a fool. E. S. Dallas, writing in 1877, recommended this good old-fashioned method: 'Scald them sufficiently with very little water till the fruit breaks. Too much water will spoil them. The water must not be thrown away, being so rich with the finest part of the fruit, that if left to stand till cold it will turn to jelly. When the gooseberries are cold, mash them all together. Passing them through a sieve or colander spoils them. The fine natural flavour which resides in the skin no art can replace . . . Sweeten with fine powdered sugar but add no nutmeg or other spice. Mix in at the last moment some rich cream, and it is ready.'

An Oldbury tart, a west of England gooseberry speciality, is rare in being made with hot water pastry. It is said that when you bite into a good tart the juice should run out.

Gooseberries are purported to have been the first bushes ever to grow in the Orkneys and Shetland, and it is said that when the inhabitants of the Shetlands read their Bibles and tried to imagine Adam hiding in the Garden of Eden all they could conjure up was a vision of a naked man cowering under a gooseberry bush. Scottish gooseberries have long been said to be 'the perfection of their race'.

Make marmalade with Seville oranges

Sevilles are the oranges you need for the hint of bitterness that a good marmalade demands. No British breakfast is truly complete without toast and marmalade.

The first recipes for orange marmalade appeared in English cookbooks in the 1600s, not as a breakfast treat but, due to the prized medicinal qualities of oranges, as a cure for indigestion. Marmalade's commercial success is owed to an incident in the early 18th century when James Keiller of Dundee bought a large quantity of Spanish oranges at a bargain price from the harbour. The fruit was discovered to be too bitter to eat, so his wife Janet decided to make them into a jam, but chopped the peel into shreds rather than crushing it to a pulp with a pestle and mortar. Her marmalade sold out overnight. By the mid-1700s the epicurean traveller Bishop Richard Pococke was describing a British breakfast for which, 'They always bring toasted bread, and besides, butter, honey and jelly of preserved orange peel.'

As well as marmalade, Sevilles make an ideal accompaniment to a gamey dish such as a rabbit casserole.

Seville or bitter oranges (*Citrus sinensis*) originate from China and were first grown in Spain and Portugal in the 12th century, having been brought to Europe by Arab traders. The crop is a short one, harvested in January. The unique quality of the fruit lies in the rind, which contains an aromatic chemical quite different from that in sweet oranges. The key to successful marmalade making is to wrap the pips and pith (which contain large amounts of pectin) in muslin and to boil them in the peel and sugar mixture.

MARMALADE FACT AND FICTION

Many stories have been told about marmalade, not all of them true:

Mary Queen of Scots, seasick with *'mer malade'* in 1561, did not give her name to a concoction given to her by a Spanish doctor.

The first marmalade was made from quinces; the name probably comes from *marmelo*, the Portuguese word for the fruit.

Oxford marmalade is named for Mrs Frank Cooper, wife of an Oxford grocer's wife who made it to her own recipe in 1874. Students loved it and nicknamed it 'Squish'.

Marmalade in cans has been taken on expeditions to the South Pole and to the top of Mount Everest.

In French cuisine a *marmelade* is a thick purée made by stewing fruit for several hours. Onions can also be cooked with sugar and balsamic vinegar to make a savoury *marmelade*.

Make the syrup before you poach your fruit

A good way of ensuring that you can cook fruit gently until it is just done, so it does not break up. As well as homemade syrups, natural ones such as maple syrup make versatile ingredients.

> According to one legend, maple syrup was discovered when a lazy wife tapped the tree rather than travelling to collect water for boiling moose meat. When she saw the sticky mess in her pot she fled, but her husband went to find her in order to compliment her on her cooking.

The secret of a good sugar syrup is to boil it long enough for plenty of water to evaporate so that the mixture becomes thick and heavy. The basic proportions are 250g (8oz) sugar to 500ml (1 pint) liquid, which can be water or water mixed with fruit juice and/or wine. For flavour you can add citrus rind, cinnamon sticks, cloves, allspice, cardamom – whatever takes your fancy. The mixture needs to be boiled for at least half an hour then is ideally cooled and strained before being used to poach fruit.

For poaching, fruit such as pears and oranges can be peeled and left whole for a pretty presentation. Fresh peaches and apricots are best halved and stoned and can be skinned before cooking: plunging them into boiling water for a couple of minutes makes the skins easier to remove.

Of all the natural syrups, maple syrup, traditionally eaten on breakfast pancakes in North America, is the best known. Centuries before Europeans introduced the honey bee to America, tribes such as the Iroquois, Algonquin and Ojibwa were adept at extracting sap from the sugar maple. They concentrated it by letting it freeze at night and chipping off the ice in the morning.

CHAPTER 5

BEAUTIFULLY BAKED

Baking is one of the great pleasures of the kitchen, and everyone appreciates home baking. Taste apart, there are few sensations to beat the touch of bread dough as you knead it or the smell of freshly baked cakes, pies or tarts as they emerge from the oven. Baking is also an art, and to be good at it demands skill, much practice and, above all, accuracy, simply because the proportions of ingredients in a mix are critical to success. Mrs Beeton summed it up like this: 'Although from puddings to pastry is but a step, it requires a higher degree of art to make the one than the other. Indeed, pastry is one of the most important branches of the culinary art.'

The time is ripe for a revival in home baking, for which modern cooks have many advantages over their forebears. Not only is it more economical, but self-raising flour is available on every supermarket shelf, for example, along with easy to blend 'instant' yeast and finely sifted icing (confectioner's) sugar, as well as plump seedless raisins and other high quality dried fruit. Ingredients can be weighed with ease on electronic scales, and ovens can not only be set to a specific temperature but are equipped with fans to ensure an even heat and a good rise. What may be less easy in a well-insulated home is to find a warm place in which to leave a yeast dough to rise – our grandmothers would simply have placed it beside the kitchen range.

You can't make bread in a cold kitchen

Unless, that is, you are making unleavened bread or a soda bread that needs no yeast. Warmth is essential to the magic of bread making: it allows the live yeast cells to multiply and produce the carbon dioxide gas that makes the mixture rise.

Bread is often called the 'staff of life', a reference to the Biblical metaphor for Christ. In St John's gospel Jesus says to his disciples: 'The bread that God gives comes down from heaven and brings life to the world,' and 'I am the bread of life. Whoever comes to me will never be hungry . . .'

Yeast (*Saccharomyces cerevisiae)* is a single-celled fungus that is fussy about warmth. Below 70°F (21°C) its cells reproduce only very slowly. Above about 130°F (56°C) they die. The temperature at which they grow fastest and most steadily is just above human body temperature, at 100°F (38°C). *Candida* yeast, which produces the lactic acid that gives sourdough bread its characteristic flavour, has similar temperature needs. The cooling of the finished loaves is as important to perfection as the cooking, because it ensures that water migrates to the crust and does not make the crumb doughy and leathery.

The apparently miraculous properties of yeast led to its medieval name of 'goddisgoode' – because it was said to have come from 'the great grace of God'.

The live yeast used for bread is the same species (though today a different variety) as that used for making beer. Ancient Egyptian women combined their breweries and bakehouses, using the waste or 'barm' from beer making to raise their bread.

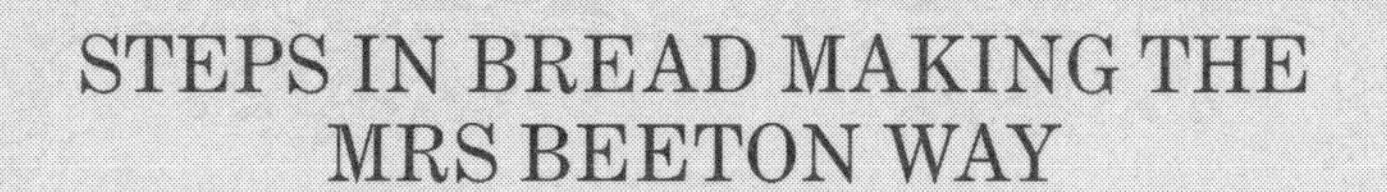

STEPS IN BREAD MAKING THE MRS BEETON WAY

The domestic guru used 1oz (25g) fresh German (compressed) yeast for every 3½lb (1.6kg) flour.

1. Mix yeast with ¾ pint (450ml) warm milk-and-water and mix until 'smooth as cream'.

2. Put the flour in a bowl with a pinch of salt and make a well in the middle. Pour in the yeast mixture and stir to make a 'thick batter in which there must be no lumps'.

3. Sprinkle plenty of flour on top and cover with a thick, clean cloth. 'Set it where the air is warm' but not 'upon the kitchen fender, for it will be too much heated there' until bubbles break through the flour.

4. Pour in a further ½ pint (300ml) warm milk-and-water. Throw on plenty of flour, then knead well 'with the knuckles of both hands' until the mixture is smooth. The dough is ready when it 'does not stick to the hands when touched'.

5. Leave to rise again, for ¾ hour. When it has swollen and is again beginning to crack, quickly cut into shapes and bake at once in a hot oven.

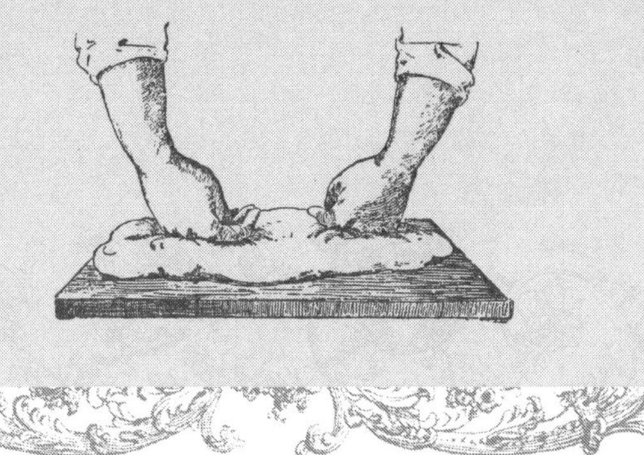

No starter, no sourdough

A saying that reveals the way in which sourdough bread is raised or leavened. This is probably the most ancient means of bread making, going back at least 6,000 years, and in some families sourdough starters, which contain wild yeasts, have been kept going for many generations.

A 'sourdough bullet' is a disparaging cowboy term for a poorly made biscuit (scone).

To make a starter or 'mother sponge', flour (either rye or wheat), water and sugar are mixed together and left in a warm place for two or three days until the mixture begins to ferment and turn sour due to the action of yeasts and bacteria from the air. This sounds easy, but the mixture also needs to be stirred frequently to provide the microbes with oxygen, and kept at around 20–25°C (86–96°F) to ensure that that they grow as vigorously as possible. The characteristic sour flavour of the bread comes from acids made as the starter matures. For wheat sourdough, the best wild yeasts are said to come from the San Francisco area of California.

To keep the starter going, cooks learned to save some of the mixture and add more water and flour to it, or to keep a little of the dough and use it to raise the next batch of bread. During the Klondike gold rush of 1898, when food was scarce and provisions more valuable than gold, it was said that a true 'Alaskan Sourdough' would rather spend a year in the hills without his rifle than try to survive without his bubbling sourdough pot. In conditions of extreme cold, miners would put a ball of dough under their clothes, next to their skin, or tuck it into their bedroll with them at night in order to keep it alive.

Bake a pizza on a stone

A saying thought to relate to a reference by Cato the Elder (234–149 BC) in his history of Rome to 'flat rounds of dough dressed with olive oil, herbs, and honey, baked on stones' and to the ancient habit in Italy of baking bread under the stones of the fire.

More important to an authentic pizza is that it should be baked in a wood-fired brick oven at a temperature of around 400°C (750°F). This degree of heat is vital to puff up the base quickly and, at the same time, to melt the mozzarella cheese usually added to the topping.

Using bread as a 'plate' was the normal way of eating in ancient times. The word *pizza* is recorded as early as AD 997 at Gatea, a port between Rome and Naples, the latter being the city destined to become the pizza capital of the world, where pizza was first sold in the street, cut in slices, from a huge tray. However it took until the end of the 19th century for the pizza to migrate, notably to the USA, where it was commonly known as tomato pie. It is said to have been introduced to Chicago by a pedlar who paraded up and down Taylor Street with a metal washtub of pizzas on his head.

The pizza could be said to have become a truly universal dish when Dean Martin sang in his 1953 hit, 'When the moon hits your eye like a big pizza pie, that's amore.'

In the *Aeneid*, the Roman poet Virgil (in Dryden's translation) refers to the ancient idea of bread as an edible platter or 'trencher':

Their homely fare dispatch'd, the hungry band
Invade their trenchers next, and soon devour,
To mend the scanty meal, their cakes of flour.
Ascanius this observ'd, and smiling said:
'See, we devour the plates on which we fed.'

Not all pizzas are flat: in a *calzone* (literally 'trouser leg') the pizza dough is folded over a filling, as in a pasty. It is also known as a *pizza ripieno*.

Pizza Margherita, made with basil, mozzarella and tomatoes (the colours of the Italian flag) was invented by the chef Raffaele Esposito in 1889 for a visit to Naples by Queen Margherita of Italy. She liked it so much that it has borne her name ever since.

MAKE HOT CROSS BUNS ON GOOD FRIDAY

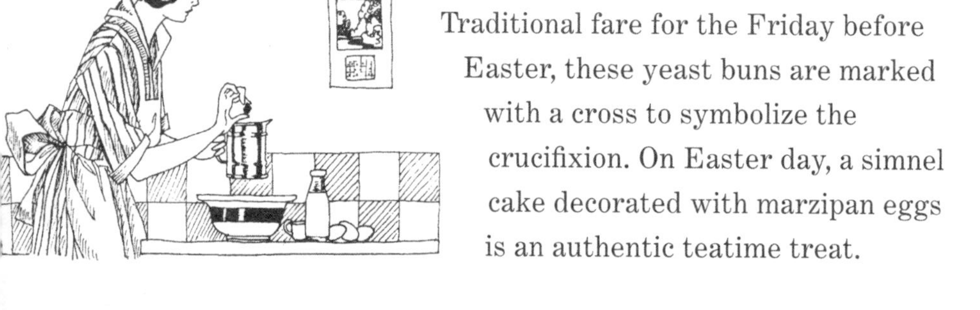

Traditional fare for the Friday before Easter, these yeast buns are marked with a cross to symbolize the crucifixion. On Easter day, a simnel cake decorated with marzipan eggs is an authentic teatime treat.

When hot cross buns were sold in city streets, vendors would use this cry:

Hot cross buns! Hot cross buns!
One a penny two a penny
Hot cross buns!
If your daughters do not like them
Give them to your sons,
But if you haven't any of these pretty elves
You cannot do better than eat them yourselves.

A rich, sweet, yeast dough with currants and spices added is the essence of the hot cross bun. The cross on top can be slashed with a knife but is more usually made from rolled-out strips of plain dough. Although the buns did not get their name until the 18th century, they almost certainly developed from the Saxon custom of marking buns with a cross to honour Eostre, the goddess of light, whose festival was adopted as Easter by early

Christians. It was believed that because of their sacred nature hot cross buns would never go mouldy, and they were habitually dried and kept as lucky charms from one year to the next.

The simnel cake is a rich fruit cake with a layer of marzipan in the centre and a marzipan topping. Small balls of marzipan are set on top and the whole grilled until lightly brown. The number of balls in the decoration can vary: some say there should be 11 to represent all the apostles but Judas Iscariot, others that there should be 12, for these 11 apostles plus Christ. Yet others maintain that 13, the total number before Good Friday, is correct.

Originally a simnel was a plain light bread that was boiled or baked and made not for Easter but for Mothering Sunday, the fourth Sunday of Lent. On this day pilgrimages were made to the cathedral, the 'mother' church of each diocese, and young girls working as servants were given the day off to visit their mothers and take as a gift a cake they had made themselves. Fruit and spices, including saffron, were 17th-century additions.

Don't open the oven door while a cake is cooking

Especially important for sponge cakes, which, like soufflés, won't rise properly if subjected to a blast of cold air. For a perfect result the oven needs to be heated to the correct temperature before the cake is put inside.

A 'true' sponge cake rises because air is whisked into it. Classic whisked fatless sponges are the Savoy, in which egg yolks are first beaten with sugar, and the egg whites then beaten

For a classic Victoria sponge, all the ingredients are the 'weight of two eggs'. Since an egg weighs about 50g (2oz), the mixture needs 100g (4oz) each of sugar, butter and flour. To get the proportions exactly right, many cooks still put the eggs on their scales instead of counterbalancing weights.

until stiff and folded in separately, and the Génoise, in which whole eggs are used. For both, flour is carefully folded in at the end of mixing.

In a creamed sponge, such as a Victoria sponge or sandwich cake, butter and caster sugar are creamed together until soft, then eggs, flour and baking powder added. When heated, the flour produces pockets of carbon dioxide in the mixture. Both this gas, and the air beaten into the cake, which expands as it is heated, will contract quickly if the oven door is opened and cold air rushes in.

Until the gas cooker made its entry into kitchens in the late 19th century, cooks were at the mercy of the range, which, although it had ventilators to help control the fierceness and heat of the fire, was hit-and-miss for cake making. Manufacturers of gas cookers were quick to produce recipe books to accompany their stoves; the 1930s *Parkinson Cookery Book* boasts that 'Cakes carefully prepared and put into a controlled oven heated to the correct temperature and given the right time cannot be failures.'

Cake when done shrinks from the pan

One of the many pieces of advice offered by Fannie Merritt Farmer. It is in most cases, she says, 'sufficient test' of doneness.

Other methods of testing are to press the top of the cake with your finger – if it springs back afterwards, the cake is cooked. For a very rich fruit cake, such as a Christmas cake, a reliable test is to insert a skewer into the centre. It will not come out clean unless the cake is cooked all through. When a cake is taken out of the oven it will continue to shrink a little and will become firmer and easier to handle if it is left in the pan for ten minutes or so before it is turned out on to a wire rack to cool.

Careful preparation of cake pans and tins is also crucial to success. Before the advent of non-stick cake tins and baking parchment for lining, tins needed to be well greased. Frugal cooks kept the wrappers from butter and lard for this purpose, although the latter were considered superior – lard was always the fat of choice for greasing pans because the salt in the butter was believed to make the mixture stick.

Miss Farmer wisely advised: 'If cake is inclined to stick, do not hurry it from the pan, but loosen with a knife around the edges and rest the pan on its four sides successively, thus by its own weight the cake may be helped out.'

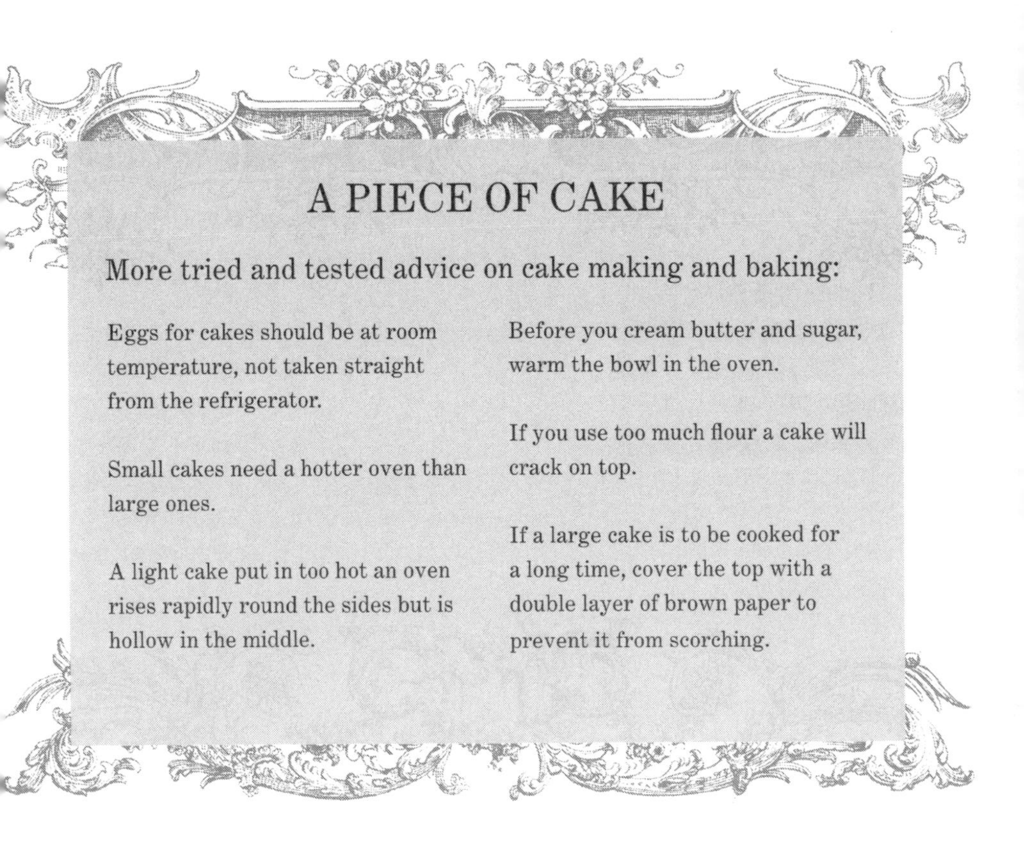

A PIECE OF CAKE

More tried and tested advice on cake making and baking:

Eggs for cakes should be at room temperature, not taken straight from the refrigerator.

Small cakes need a hotter oven than large ones.

A light cake put in too hot an oven rises rapidly round the sides but is hollow in the middle.

Before you cream butter and sugar, warm the bowl in the oven.

If you use too much flour a cake will crack on top.

If a large cake is to be cooked for a long time, cover the top with a double layer of brown paper to prevent it from scorching.

Stop cherries from sinking: roll them in flour

Good advice when making a cake with glacé cherries, but not infallible – and some cooks swear that ground almonds work even better. Washing the cherries to get rid of excess sugar on their surface can also help to keep them evenly distributed through the cake.

The problem with cherries is that they are the heaviest ingredients in the cake mix. Rolling them in flour or almonds helps to suspend them in the mixture while it 'sets' in the oven. Another good tip is to use a moderate oven so that the cake batter solidifies quite quickly, thus ensuring that at least some of the cherries stay at the top and in the middle.

Keeping summer fruit for winter use by preserving it with sugar has a long history. The Roman cookbook *Apicius* proposes, for a variety of fruit: 'Select them all very carefully with the stems on and place them in honey so that they do not touch each other.' The substitution of sugar for honey probably began around 1600. The French have perfected the crystallizing or candying process, cooking the stoned fruit lightly before immersing it in syrup and draining it daily, concentrating the sugar mixture until the correct texture is achieved.

The sweet, sticky coating of glacé cherries is produced by dipping the candied fruit in concentrated sugar syrup.

Cherries, which can either be fresh or preserved in brandy, have no chance of sinking when they are used with cream as a filling in a German classic, the Black Forest cherry cake. The cake was invented in 1915 by pastry chef Josef Keller at the Café Ahrend (now called Café Agner) in Bad Godesberg. Keller's original recipe was passed to August Schaefer, the apprentice in Keller's own establishment in Radolfzell, which he opened after the end of World War I.

For a Swiss roll, speed is the essence

A swift touch is essential for successfully finishing this cake, also called a sponge roll or jelly roll. Similarly, a roulade of any kind needs quick, deft rolling to prevent it from splitting and to ensure a perfect finish.

The Swiss roll is made by cooking a fatless sponge cake mixture in a shallow, oblong tin. As Mary Harrison prescribes in *The Skilful Cook* of 1919, the secret is to 'Have a baking-tin ready greased with butter, and lined with greased paper. Pour in the mixture; spread it over and bake it till a light fawn colour. Then turn it on to a cloth. Spread with the jam melted and roll up quickly.' For a superior finish the cake can be turned out on to a piece of greaseproof paper well dusted with caster or icing sugar.

The *bûche de Noël* is an edible version of the log originally burned at Christmas – an echo of the pagan midwinter festival of Yule.

The French seasonal speciality the *bûche de Noël* or Yule log is a chocolate-based version of the Swiss roll. This is made with a sheet of Génoise cake pastry – a rich mixture with ground almonds added – spread with buttercream and rolled into a log shape. The outside is then decorated with a chocolate or coffee buttercream applied with an icing bag and nozzle, or roughened with a fork so as to look like tree bark.

A roulade can be anything from a rolled meringue to a spinach roulade, in which the roll is made from a mixture of eggs and cooked spinach and filled with a creamy cheese mixture. *Larousse Gastronomique* of 1961 gives a different definition of a roulade as a 'rolled piece of veal or pork . . . spread with some kind of forcemeat and rolled into a sausage.' It says that the term 'is also applied to various preparations, mostly of pork or veal, made like galantines'. Popular versions today are *brachiole* or, in Italy, *involtini*, in which thin slices of beef, pork or chicken are rolled around a filling of Parmesan, eggs, mushrooms and other ingredients and served in a sauce such as tomato.

Make gingerbread with molasses

Sensible advice for the modern cook, although the original gingerbread was not a true cake but a mixture of honey, breadcrumbs and ginger. Molasses, or black treacle, a by-product of sugar refining, became common only in the 17th century.

Ginger has been used as a flavouring in Europe since Roman times, and by the late Middle Ages it was almost as widely available as pepper, which helps to explain why gingerbread has such a long history. There are many variations on the basic recipe. Some versions are more like biscuits (cookies), others more like cake. Grasmere gingerbread, a speciality of the English Lake District, resembles shortbread, while Ashbourne gingerbread is pale in colour and made with sugar, not molasses. Like shortbread, gingerbread was commonly made in decorative moulds and, because it was sold at country fairs, was known as a 'fairing'. Parkin, a north of England speciality made with oatmeal, is another variation on the gingerbread theme.

The old custom of making gingerbread men links to the folktale of the man-shaped cake that comes to life in an old woman's kitchen and runs away. As a variety of animals try to eat him, he replies with the line, 'I ran away from an old woman, and I can run away from you, I can,' but when he meets the fox, despite listing everyone he has evaded, he gets eaten up in one gulp. Gingerbread men are still popular and in England are traditionally made to eat on Bonfire Night, 5 November, the celebration of the demise of Guy Fawkes.

John Adams, president of the United States from 1797 to 1801, declared molasses, used to manufacture rum, to be 'an essential ingredient in American independence', because the British had slapped high duties on it, then made it illegal for the colonists to buy it from their enemies the French.

The saying 'To take the gilt off the gingerbread' means to deprive something of its attraction but derives from the medieval practice of decorating gingerbread with box leaves set in a fleur de lis pattern. Cloves, with their heads decorated with gilt, were then pushed in like nails.

Doughnuts must be deep fried

The only proper way to cook a doughnut (or donut) which for authenticity should also be sprinkled with fine sugar. The original doughnut is thought to have been a solid sphere, with no hole in the middle.

Doughnuts were a European invention, probably attributable to the Germans, although it was the Dutch who, as settlers, took them to America. The author Washington Irving, writing in the early 19th century and describing the table of Dutch immigrants in New Amsterdam (later New York), said that it boasted 'an enormous dish of balls of sweetened dough, fried in hog's fat, and called dough nuts or oly keks'. By the middle of the century it had become the custom to make a hole in the centre of the dough to create a ring. An American homewares catalogue of 1870 included a doughnut cutter.

The dough for a doughnut, made with flour, sugar and milk, has either baking powder or yeast added. Beaten eggs are optional. The dough needs to contain enough water that when it is plunged into the fat it quickly turns to steam, which puffs the doughnuts up. Spherical doughnuts often have a little jam inserted in the centre.

Doughnut variations include *pampushky* – a Christmas doughnut from the Ukraine filled with jam or poppy seeds – and *rosquilla*, a ring-shaped Spanish doughnut flavoured with anise and dusted with icing sugar and cinnamon.

Doughnuts were once foods for festivals and special occasions but became everyday fare with the arrival of brands such as Krispy Kreme, all-American doughnuts now also available in Britain. In 1937 Vernon Rudolph bought a secret recipe from a French chef in New Orleans and began selling doughnuts to local grocery stores from a rented building in Salem, North Carolina. So many people stopped by to ask for them that he cut a hole in the wall and started selling his Hot Original Glazed doughnuts directly to customers.

For pastry: cool while making, hot while baking

Undoubtedly the key to success with everyday shortcrust or 'plain' pastry, and for flaky and puff pastry. The exceptions are fancy pastries such as choux and hot-water crusts. Large Victorian kitchens had separate pastry rooms with cool marble tops, which were a boon to cooks in the summer months.

In making shortcrust pastry, coolness is vital to prevent sticky gluten in the flour from developing and to keep the particles of fat (lard, butter or a mixture of the two) from becoming liquid and thus too evenly distributed through the mixture. To keep everything as cool as possible, use chilled fat, cut it into the flour with a knife, then rub it in with the fingertips. Quickly stir in chilled water with a knife, and finish the mixing using the fingers of one hand until the dough just leaves the sides of the bowl. Half an hour's rest in the refrigerator, followed by rolling of the dough on a cool worktop – ideally of marble – are the other essentials for avoiding unwanted heat. For a shiny finish, pastry can be glazed with beaten egg. For a deep brown colour, just the yolk is used; for a pale effect both egg yolk and white are mixed, with a little sugar added for a sweet dish.

To distinguish savoury pies from sweet ones after cooking and before they were brought to the table the former were traditionally decorated with pastry leaves and other embellishments.

In a hot oven (180°C/350°F/Gas 4) the particles of fat or shortening melt, but because they are separate from the flour, also prevent heavy gluten forming. Quick, high temperature cooking also keeps the starch grains in the flour stiff, making the pastry crisp. This, combined with the expansion of air trapped in the mixture and the release of steam as the water in it evaporates, gives the pastry its lightness.

Puff pastry is made by folding pastry in layers, with butter added between each. Coolness is essential during preparation, but the finished dough, composed of up to 240 layers, needs very high heat (420°F/220°C/Gas 7) to expand the air trapped in the layers as quickly as possible, and to make the pastry crisp and golden.

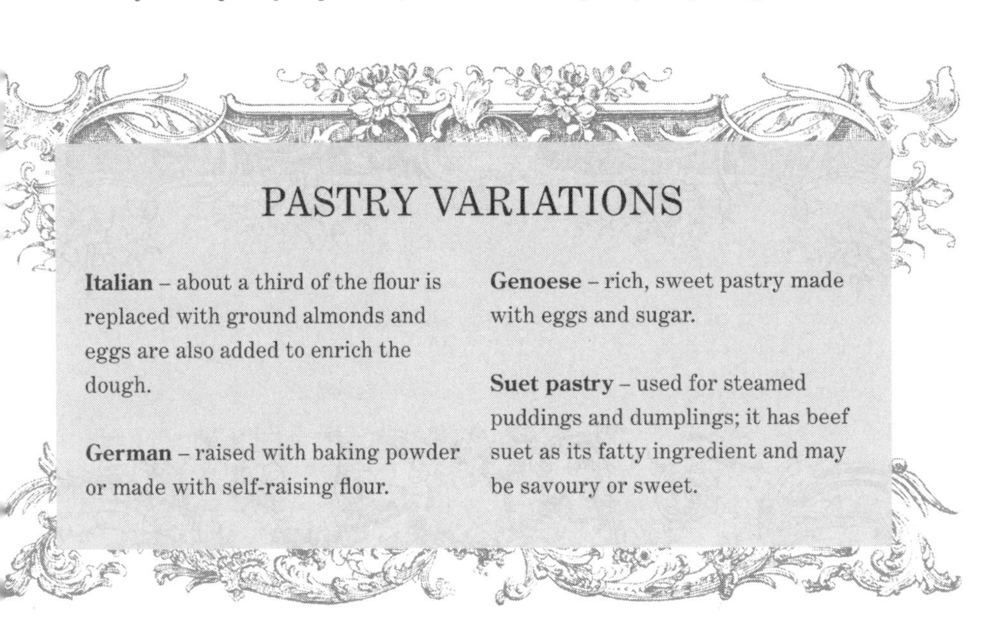

PASTRY VARIATIONS

Italian – about a third of the flour is replaced with ground almonds and eggs are also added to enrich the dough.

German – raised with baking powder or made with self-raising flour.

Genoese – rich, sweet pastry made with eggs and sugar.

Suet pastry – used for steamed puddings and dumplings; it has beef suet as its fatty ingredient and may be savoury or sweet.

Side rolling makes pastry rise unevenly

The quality of rolling is key to success with both shortcrust and puff pastry. It needs to be evenly done over the whole of the paste and quickly carried out in order to keep the pastry cool and to prevent it from stretching so that it does not shrink as it cooks.

Flouring the board and the rolling pin are also essential to stop the pastry sticking, and ideally it should be rolled in just one direction. A wooden rolling pin, which should have fixed, not revolving, handles, is traditional, but marble or glass will help to keep the pastry extra cool. Cooks of old would fill their glass pins with cold water.

Glass rolling pins were often given as gifts to sailors and hung in ships' cabins for luck. These might bear mottoes such as: 'From rocks and sands and barren lands/Kind fortune keep me free,/And from great guns and women's tongues/Good Lord deliver me.' Also for good fortune, and made of blue glass, they were presented as wedding gifts.

Rolling is a key to making puff pastry, for which the basic ingredients are simply equal weights of plain flour and butter. The aim is to achieve layers, each as thin as a sheet of notepaper. Mrs E. W. Kirk, using 225g (½lb) of each, as well as an egg yolk, a teaspoon of lemon juice, salt and cold water, gives an easy method in her 1924 *Tried Favourites Cookery Book*: '. . . put the flour into a bowl, add the salt, make a hole in the centre, and water enough to mix to a firm paste. Work until smooth, then roll it out thinly, place the butter on one half of the paste, fold the other, and press the edges together. Let it stand in a cool place 15 minutes; now roll it out into a long piece, fold in three,

'There be some that to this paste add sugar but it is certain to hinder the rising thereof.' (Anonymous, on puff pastry, around 1600.)

turn the edges towards you, roll again, fold in three and set aside for another 15 minutes. Repeat this till the paste has been rolled six times since adding the butter. The seventh time the paste must be rolled to the required thickness.'

A TARTE TATIN SERVED COLD HAS NO MERITS

Because this dessert needs to be warm enough to ensure that when crème fraîche or whipped cream is added at the table it melts immediately on contact. The dish owes its origins to two French sisters from Lamotte-Beuvron.

The original version of this upside-down tart was made with apples, but now other fruits, such as apricots, pears and pineapple, and even savoury ingredients such as onion, have become acceptable. A *tarte tatin* is made by covering the base of a pan with a mixture of melted butter and lightly cooked sugar, then adding sliced apples and topping the whole with puff pastry. As it cooks the butter and sugar caramelize, so that when the tart is inverted on to a serving plate this becomes the topping. Firm dessert apples that keep their shape are essential; cookers become too mushy for a good result.

The trickiest part of the cooking is the turning out. After it comes out of the oven the *tarte* needs to be left for ten minutes. You then run a small, sharp knife around the edge to loosen it and place a large plate over the pan. Holding plate and pan together using oven gloves or tea towels, you quickly but carefully invert the dessert on to the plate.

The full name of this dish is *La tarte des Demoiselles Tatin*, which reflects its invention by Caroline and Stéphanie Tatin, who ran a hotel in the Sologne region of France. The story goes that one day in 1889 Stéphanie, the sister who did most of the cooking, started to make a

It is said that *tarte tatin* became universally popular only when it reached Maxim's in Paris after the restaurateur Louis Vaudable had tasted it at the sisters' establishment.

traditional apple pie but forgot to check on the fruit cooking in butter and sugar, which began to burn. She quickly put the pastry on top and shoved the dish in the oven. When she turned it out she discovered that she had a delicious dessert.

Beat choux pastry until it leaves the sides of the pan

Totally different from other types of pastry, choux is a cross between a batter and a dough. One of the secrets of success lies in beating eggs and air into it.

The way in which choux pastry is made involves cooking it twice – once on the top of the stove and once in the oven. A basic mixture is 75g (2¾oz) plain flour, a pinch of salt, 50g (1¾oz) diced butter and two eggs, beaten. The flour is first sifted on to a large sheet of greaseproof paper then the butter is put into a pan with 150ml (5fl oz) water and brought slowly to a rolling ball. You then take the pan off the heat, tip in the flour and beat it until it leaves the sides of the pan. The egg is added a little at a time, the mixture being beaten well at each addition until the paste is glossy and has a dropping consistency.

The finished paste can be spooned in small heaps on to a greased baking sheet or, for éclairs, put into a piping bag and shaped into oblongs. After baking them in a hot oven (220°C/425°F/Gas 7) for 20–25 minutes, it is wise to make a small slit in each to let the hot air escape and to prevent the insides from going soggy. When cooled, the classic éclair filling is sweetened whipped cream and the topping is a chocolate or coffee icing (frosting).

The word choux, *French for cabbage, refers to the cabbage-shaped balls into which the pastry is often formed.*

It is said that in 1533, when Catherine de Medici left Florence to marry the Duke of Orléans, she took to France her entire Italian court, including her chefs. In 1540, her head chef, Panterelli, invented a hot, dried paste with which he made a gateau. He christened it *pâte à Panterelli* although later it became known as *pâte à popelini* (*popelins* were cakes made in the Middle Ages in the shape of women's breasts). In around 1760 the making of choux paste, as it subsequently became known, was improved by a *chef de patisserie* named Jean Avice, who allegedly created the first profiteroles. The recipe used today was perfected by Antonin Carême, one of the foremost chefs of the late 19th century.

CHOUX DELIGHTS

More superb dishes that can be made with choux pastry:

Profiteroles – miniature choux pastry buns, which can be sweet (as in cream puffs) or filled with a savoury mixture. For weddings in France they are piled into a tall cone-shaped *croquembouche*, covered in spun sugar.

Gougère – a Burgundian speciality, a savoury 'cake' of choux pastry (often flavoured with cheese) filled with a mixture such as a salpiçon of cooked chicken and ham with softened onion, mushrooms and herbs added.

Beignets – small deep-fried choux buns, filled with jam or a savoury mixture. The paste may be flavoured with cheese, herbs, spices or citrus zest, or have dried fruits added. In France small, plain round beignets are crudely nicknamed *pets de nonnes* or 'nuns' farts'.

Let the steam out of a pie with a funnel

For a pie made with pastry, undoubtedly the best way of helping to ensure that the top does not sag and get soggy as the mixture inside heats up. Pie funnels are small ceramic 'chimneys' placed in the centre of a deep pie, poking through the pastry lid. They can be plain or, reminiscent of the nursery rhyme, made in the shape of blackbirds, but they are also available as gnomes, chess pieces and other designs.

The making of pies has more than one association with birds, apart from the rhyme that begins:

Sing a song of sixpence,
A pocket full of rye
Four and twenty blackbirds,
Baked in a pie.

When the pie was opened
The birds began to sing
Was not that a dainty dish
To set before a king.

It has also been postulated that the word 'pie' comes from magpie because, just as this bird will pick up and collect almost anything, so a pie can contain any number of ingredients. Another theory is that the word is derived from *les petits pieds*, the French for small birds such as quails and ortolans, which were frequently baked in pies.

Pies are now small compared with those of earlier times. One of the biggest ever recorded was made in Egypt in the 12th century. The pastry alone was made with 13.6kg (30lb) of flour. Among the many ingredients were 20 fowls, 20 chickens and 50 smaller birds, some of them baked and stuffed with eggs or meat. Early pies always had pastry on top and underneath, but the word can now mean any dish with a separate topping, not necessarily of pastry, such as the potato on a fish pie, or meringue on a key lime pie.

Regarding the quality and quantity of pies, Maria Parloa in 1887 complains: 'Unfortunately some housekeepers make pies every week in the year, and they and their families would feel lost if a day passed without the usual quantity of pie. Wiser housekeepers have pies only occasionally, and when the fruits and vegetables of which they are made are at their best.'

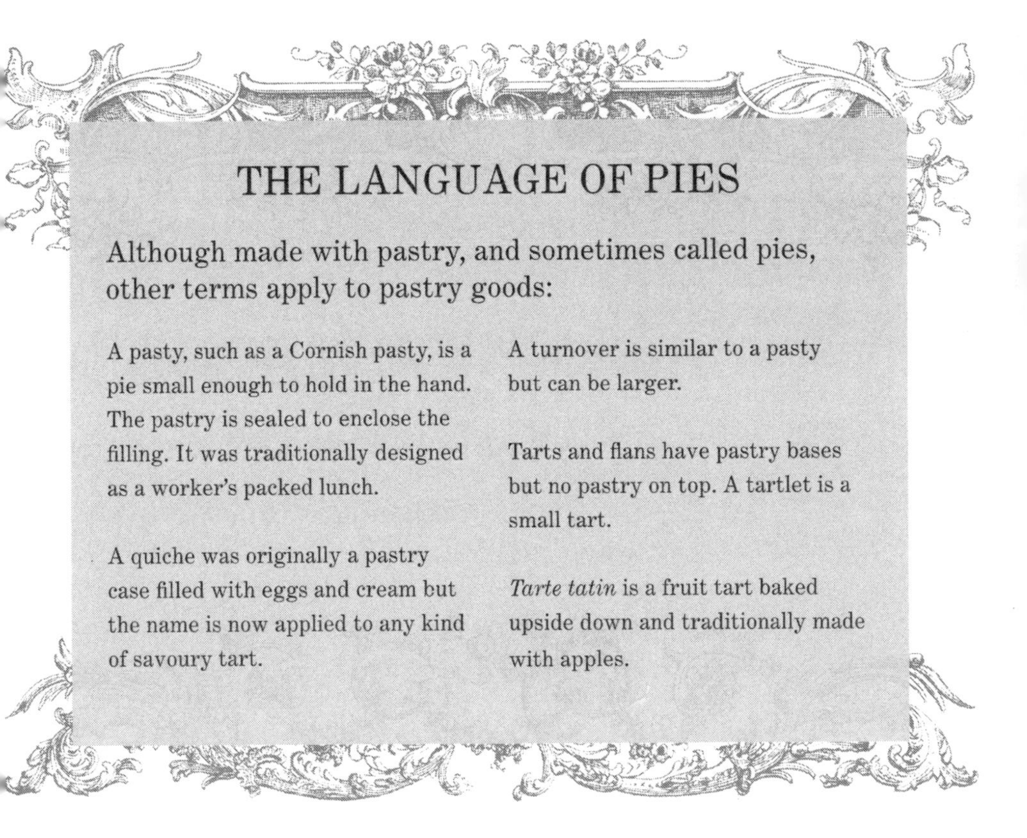

THE LANGUAGE OF PIES

Although made with pastry, and sometimes called pies, other terms apply to pastry goods:

A pasty, such as a Cornish pasty, is a pie small enough to hold in the hand. The pastry is sealed to enclose the filling. It was traditionally designed as a worker's packed lunch.

A quiche was originally a pastry case filled with eggs and cream but the name is now applied to any kind of savoury tart.

A turnover is similar to a pasty but can be larger.

Tarts and flans have pastry bases but no pastry on top. A tartlet is a small tart.

Tarte tatin is a fruit tart baked upside down and traditionally made with apples.

A raised pie needs hot-water pastry

This is definitely the type of pastry needed for a pork or game pie, also known as a standing pie, but is no longer within the repertoire of most ordinary cooks. The pastry case was once – from its purpose and its thick, robust nature – known as a coffin.

The porkpie hat, a 19th-century variation on the fedora, was named from its flat-topped shape.

The secret of making hot-water pastry lies in getting it to exactly the right texture and handling it well. When it works, the process is enormously rewarding. The proportions required are 450g (1lb) each of lard and flour to 450ml (1 pint) water and a generous amount of salt. First the water and lard are boiled together, then the flour and salt are added and the resulting stiff paste is kneaded to a smooth dough. It is then set aside in a warm place for half an hour, covered with a warm cloth.

Once the meat is prepared, Mrs Loudon, writing in 1851, instructs her readers: 'A piece of the paste large enough to form one pie is broken off . . . When it is just the right heat to bear being moulded, and yet to retain whatever shape may be given to it, the piece of paste is worked with the hands on a pasteboard, into the form of a high-peaked hat with a broad brim; then the peak of the hat being turned downwards on the board one of the hands is put inside the hat, and the other is used to raise and smooth the sides, till the pie is gradually worked into a proper shape. The meat is then put into the crust in layers, two of lean and one of fat, and pressed as closely as possible, in order that the pie may cut firm when cold.'

This might sound easy enough, but cooks would also use wooden moulds to give pies their shape, or roll out the pastry and use it to line metal moulds. It is easy to distinguish pies made in moulds – they have smooth straight sides compared with the typically baggy appearance of hand-raised pies. However made, the edges around the top need to be crimped.

When the filling for the pie was pork, this could be salt or fresh. Seasoning is now usually exclusively savoury, unlike this 14th-century recipe: 'Flea [kill] Pyg and cut him in pieces, season with pepper and salt, and nutmeg, and large mace, and lay in your coffin good store of raisins and currants, and fill with sweet butter and close it and serve hot or cold.'

A SOUFFLÉ COOKED TOO FAST WILL BE FULL OF HOLES

The art of the hot soufflé comes down to confident mixing, careful cooking and immediate serving. When it succeeds, few dishes are more spectacular or delicious.

Soufflé is a French word meaning 'puffed up' and the dish is indeed a French concoction of the late 18th century. It was served as a savoury at the end of a dinner or as a light luncheon, but was also considered an ideal – and safe – dish for an invalid.

The cheese soufflé is the classic savoury version; hot chocolate, lemon and fruit the sweet equivalents. A cold soufflé, set with gelatine, is more like a mousse.

The scientific secret behind the soufflé lies in the creation of a foam of stiffly beaten egg whites, which is folded into a sauce made from butter, flour and the yolks. When this mixture is heated two things happen. The air trapped

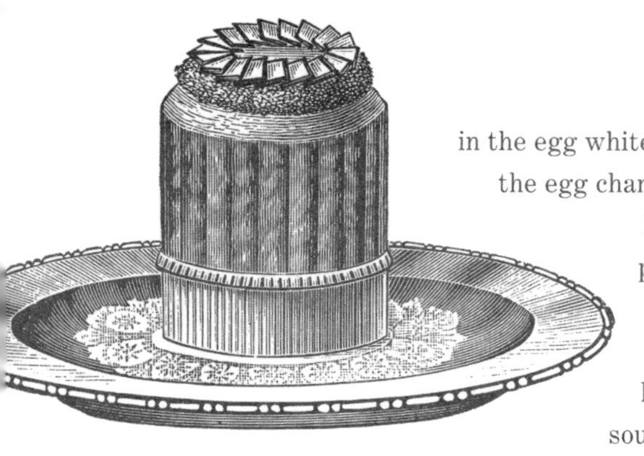

in the egg white foam expands and the proteins in the egg change from liquid to solid – they set. In the perfect soufflé the setting point and the moment of maximum expansion of the foam coincide. If the oven is too hot setting will happen too quickly, creating a solid soufflé full of holes. If it is too cold the centre will not set properly and be too liquid. An ideal oven setting is 350°F/180°C/Gas 4. To prevent a soufflé cooking too quickly, place the dish in a pan of hot water, to come about halfway up, before you put it in the oven.

Resist, above all, the temptation to open the oven door while the dish is cooking. A rush of cold air will prevent the air in the soufflé from expanding properly. Equally, a soufflé left standing once it is out of the oven will quickly begin to collapse as the air inside it cools and contracts.

A soufflé can also be a chilled dessert made with whipped cream and fruit and set with gelatine. Once set it may be elaborately decorated.

Shortbread must be made with salted butter

Salted butter is guaranteed to bring a full flavour to traditional Scottish shortbread. It is still possible to find the wooden moulds once used to shape and flute the dough. Triangular 'petticoat tails' are thought to date from the 12th century, if not earlier.

Shortbread gets its name from the 'short cakes' of the 16th century, the word 'short' describing the small size of these items, not the fat or 'shortening' with which they are made. Because the ingredients are so few – simply 100g (4oz) plain flour, 25g (1oz) caster sugar and 50g (2oz) melted butter, mixed and

kneaded together – their quality is essential. For a slightly different taste and a desirable, slightly gritty texture, the Scots frequently replace a quarter of the wheat flour with rice flour.

Petticoat tails are created by forming shortbread into a round shape, marking it into triangles and cutting a small hole from the centre. The result is triangles with curved, not pointed ends. The name is believed to come not from undergarments but from 'petty cotes tallis': 'petty' meant small, 'cotes' were small enclosures (such as sheep pens) and 'tallis' were cuts or any kind of cut-out pattern.

Shortbread was once a festive food and could have extra ingredients added. In 1826 a Scotswoman, Meg Dods, wrote of adding almonds, extra butter and candied citrus peel to shortbread she was sending 'as a holiday present to England'.

A shortcake is similar to shortbread but usually has baking powder added, which gives a softer, more cake-like result.

Similar to shortbread are Goosnargh cakes, a Whitsuntide speciality originating in a village of this name near Preston, Lancashire. They are flavoured with caraway seeds and, unusually, coriander.

CHAPTER 6

THE CAREFUL COOK

Compared with the austerity of wartime rations, or the days when a family killed a pig in the autumn and smoked or salted it to make it last right through the winter, food is now plentiful. But as prices rise and the world becomes aware of potential scarcities, thrift is once more the watchword of the kitchen. Our grandparents had plenty to say about care in the kitchen – and of necessity practised what they preached. They made jams and pickles, kept and ate every scrap of meat from a roast joint, and used the bones and trimmings as the basis for making stocks and soups. Absolutely nothing was wasted. Vegetables and fruit grown in the garden were bottled or dried, or made into wine. On grand estates, before the advent of the deep freeze, perishables were kept in ice houses for use through the winter.

The careful cook keeps an eye on planning, timing and budget. In her 'hints to young housekeepers' Mary Harrison, writing in 1919 with the less well off in mind, gives advice that applies equally well today: 'Take every pains to know how to judge of the quality of meat, groceries, &c., so that you may not be imposed on.' She also reminds her readers of the nutritional value of dried vegetables: 'Even some vegetable produces, rich in nitrogen, as haricot beans,' she says, 'may be used in the same way as meat or cheese, and for the same purpose. It is a pity,' she adds, 'that the value of haricot beans, pea, lentils and oatmeal is not more generally known . . . macaroni and semolina are also valuable foods.'

Stop pasta sticking: add a spoonful of oil to the cooking water

A wise precaution for fresh pasta, which tends to be stickier than the dried variety, though a method that is despised by professionals. All pasta is less likely to stick if it is cooked in plenty of salted water.

For cooking allow, as a rule of thumb, 3 litres (7 pints) of water and a tablespoon of salt for every 450g (1lb) of dried pasta, with an extra 1 litre (1¾ pints) for every additional 225g (8oz). Plunging the pasta into this generous amount of boiling water will allow it to come quickly to the boil, help the pieces to stay separate and give it enough room to swell.

It is said that spaghetti is ready to eat when it will stick in place if thrown at the wall, but more conventionally it should be timed to be *al dente*, or with bite. Literally the expression means 'to the tooth'. This may take up to 12 minutes for dried pasta but only three for fresh.

Marco Polo, who returned to Venice from his travels to the East in 1298, did not introduce pasta to Italy. The evidence: a 'basketful of macaroni' listed in the estate of one Ponzio Bastone in 1279. That this was obviously dried pasta, not fresh, proves, say food historians, that pasta making already had a long tradition there. In fact pasta was probably 'invented' independently by both the ancient Chinese and the Etruscans in about the 4th century BC.

Macaroni was almost certainly the first pasta enjoyed in the West. Macaroni cheese, still the ultimate comfort food, featured in British recipe books from the Middle Ages onwards. And though Spanish settlers had brought pasta to America, Thomas Jefferson was so delighted by the macaroni that he ate in Paris in the 1780s that he brought two crates back home with him. The song by Edward Bangs, first printed in England in 1778 and in America in 1794 (though possibly sung by British troops in the Anglo-French conflict of 1755–63), is testament to the vogue for pasta:

Yankee Doodle came to town
Riding on a pony
Stuck a feather in his cap
And called it Macaroni.

It was around this time that 'macaroni' came to mean a fop or dandy – a reference to all the young men returning from their tours of Europe who eagerly affected Italian accents and fashions.

MANY SHAPES AND SIZES

Of the dozens of different pasta shapes made commercially, some have wonderfully descriptive Italian names that relate to their shapes:

Capelli d'angelo – angel hair or little hairs – the thinnest spaghetti.

Capelletti – small hats – pasta twisted into shapes like three-cornered hats.

Farfalle – resembling butterflies.

Linguine di passero – sparrows' tongues – thin, oval spaghetti.

Maltagliati – badly cut – narrow diamond or triangular shapes.

Orecchiette – little ears – shaped as their name describes.

Vermicelli – small worms – thin spaghetti, but not as thin as angel hair.

Lumache – snail-shaped shells.

A FRUGAL COOK KEEPS HER GIBLETS

And uses them to make gravy to accompany her roast fowl, or stock for soup. The liver, however, which can impart a bitter taste, is best cooked separately. After a bird has been roasted or boned the careful cook will also boil up the carcass. If it is not needed immediately the resulting stock freezes well.

The word 'giblet' comes from the old French *gibelet*, meaning a stew of game birds. The innards were once made into giblet pies. Mrs Beeton recommends adding rump steak to a set of duck or goose giblets.

As well as the innards of the bird – heart, neck and gizzard – the cook may add any trimmings such as the ends of the legs and pieces of skin to the giblet pot. Onions and other vegetables such as mushrooms, carrots and celery are essential to the flavour of the stock, plus some herbs. Boiling up giblets is also a good way of using up woody pieces of vegetables, stalks from mushrooms, parsley and the like, as they are packed with flavour and will be discarded once the stock is strained.

There are lots of ways of cooking chicken, duck and turkey livers. Simply fried with a little onion and sage and served on toast, they are an excellent snack. Writing in his *Dictionary* in the late 17th century John Knott suggests that the cook should 'Set a saucepan on the fire with melted bacon, butter, mushrooms, truffles, and morils [morels] . . . season with salt, pepper and a faggot [bunch] of sweet herbs and toss them up together; then moisten them with gravy, and let them simmer a while; when they are about half done, put in your livers, then stew.'

Save sponge cake for a trifle

A trifle is a great way to use up stale sponge cake, although it can also be made with ratafias or other biscuits that have a softer cake-like texture. For a genuine old-fashioned trifle, sherry is an obligatory ingredient.

Trifle as we know it today is a dish that has its origins in the mid-18th century. According to early cookery books it was made by putting biscuits in the base of a bowl, soaking them in wine and covering them with custard or syllabub.

By the Victorian era, cake and cream were used, as in this recipe of the 1870s: 'Mix early in the day a quart of good cream with six ounces of sifted sugar, a glass of sherry, the juice and zest of a lemon, and a little cinnamon. Whip it well and put the froth, as it rises, on a reversed sieve to drain. As the time draws near for using the trifle put some sponge cakes, ratafias, and the like on a deep glass or crystal dish. Moisten them well with sherry, grate the zest of a lemon on them, and add a layer of raspberry or strawberry jam. Pour over them a goodly quantity of thick custard; heap over this the whipt cream; and ornament it with colour – petals of flowers, harlequin confits, or streaks of red jelly.'

In Italy a trifle is known as a *zuppa inglese* (literally 'English soup'), a name said to derive from the fact that the dish became popular there when it arrived in Florence with English settlers in the 19th century.

President Andrew Jackson's trifle, named for his liking of the dessert, is made with almond macaroons and orange marmalade. Both the macaroons and the whipped cream used for the topping are flavoured with sweet sherry.

EVEN STALE BREAD HAS ITS USES

Many uses, in fact, from making stuffing for a chicken to a delicious apple charlotte or bread and butter pudding. Breadcrumbs freeze very well, and the careful cook will keep a supply in the freezer.

Stale bread, especially good white bread, is a most versatile ingredient. Cut thinly, it is much better than fresh bread for lining a bowl when making a summer pudding and, with dried fruit and an egg custard, is the basis for a bread and butter pudding (for which stale brioche or panettone are best of all).

Rusks for babies were once made by putting pieces from the crust of a stale loaf in the oven to dry. For a bedtime snack in wartime, children would be given bread and milk.

A stuffing or forcemeat is made from breadcrumbs mixed with everything from onions and herbs to minced meats and chopped nuts. As well as being used inside a bird or a piece of rolled meat it can also be made into forcemeat balls, the traditional accompaniment for dishes such as jugged hare (see page 56). These are always well flavoured and may also contain suet, which gives them a texture more like that of a dumpling.

For making breadcrumbs, stale bread was once grated or worked with the hands. The advent of the food processor has made this much less of a chore. For dry breadcrumbs, used to coat fried food such as an escalope, they need to be cooked in the oven until brown then rubbed again to make them very fine. Either fresh or dried, breadcrumbs also make a good topping in place of potato for baked dishes such as a fish pie.

The magazine *Home Chat* for 25 April 1896, under the heading 'Economical Household Cookery', suggested breadcrumbs as the basis for 'A Nice Breakfast or Lunch Dish': 'Take half a pound of bread-crumbs; mix with them a quarter of a pound of cold, chopped ham, or lean bacon, or any cold meat. Add two teaspoonfuls of chopped parsley and onion, salt and pepper, and about three-quarters of a pint of stock to well moisten it. Turn all into a greased pie-dish. Cover the top with bread-crumbs. Break a few tiny bits of butter on the top, and bake about half an hour. Sprinkle the top with finely-chopped parsley and serve hot.'

THRIFTY BUT DELICIOUS

Some more ways with bread and breadcrumbs:

Lemon dumplings – made with breadcrumbs, suet, sugar and lemon rind mixed with egg and milk.

Panada – stale bread soaked in water, squeezed dry then beaten with caraway, cinnamon, nutmeg, lemon zest, milk, egg and sugar to make a drink.

Keokuk toast – slices of stale bread dipped in a pancake batter mixture and fried.

Pancotto – Italian soup with bread, chilli, garlic and parsley in a good stock, served with pecorino cheese.

Brown bread pudding – bread soaked in boiling milk, strained and mixed with brown sugar, eggs, raisins, lemon zest and vanilla, then steamed.

Bread ice cream – a frozen mixture of breadcrumbs with cream, sugar and egg yolks flavoured with vanilla.

Choose cheese by its texture and taste

Because no cheese can be judged solely on its looks, despite the wise words of the poet T. S. Eliot that you should 'Never commit yourself to a cheese without having first *examined* it.'

Ideally, cheese needs to be tasted at room temperature, not direct from the refrigerator, and also judged by its aroma. The mix of sensations you experience will depend on the milk from which the cheese has been made, the microorganisms involved in its creation and the time and method of maturation.

Cheese was almost certainly first made by accident, probably when milk was carried in 'bags' made from animal stomachs, where it came in contact with traces of rennet.

Cheese is unbeatable eaten on its own, and as anything from a snack to a course in its own right. When serving varieties such as Brie and Camembert, perfect ripeness, judged as a soft centre on the point of becoming liquid, is essential. For blue cheeses such as Stilton, key qualities are a blend of 'bite' and a creaminess of texture.

Cheese is an essential ingredient in many cooked dishes and must be chosen accordingly. To ensure good melting, a cheese needs a high fat content but must not be too hard. A Gruyère or Spanish Manchego cheese

satisfies these criteria, as does a mozzarella when used, for example, as a pizza topping. For a cheese sauce, a mature Cheddar or a similar hard cheese is a good choice – its bite will diminish when added to a béchamel mixture. A mild cheese such as a cottage cheese or a ricotta is perfect for a cheesecake, while to top a pasta dish, freshly grated Parmesan is the cheese of choice (see page 29.)

An old way of storing cheese was to rub the exterior with butter to make it airtight and so exclude the agents of decay.

Never cook a green potato

This is a case of 'green for danger', because the green colour betrays the presence of poisonous alkaloids. Similar substances found in other plants include nicotine in tobacco, caffeine in coffee and morphine, the juice of the opium poppy.

The chemicals that give potatoes their great flavour can also make them unsafe to eat. White potato flesh contains small amounts of the alkaloids solanine and chaconine, but when the tubers – especially small, young ones – are exposed to light, or are stored at too high or too low a temperature, alkaloid levels increase, producing green patches. Moreover, these chemicals are not destroyed by heat and, if eaten in quantity, create a burning sensation on the tongue, rather like pepper, which can be followed by collapse.

To be safe, a green potato should be discarded, though you may find that the green coloration extends only a little way beneath the skin. However, to get maximum nutrition from potatoes they are best cooked and eaten unpeeled. As well as the benefits of fibre in the outermost layer, most of the vitamin C potatoes contain is situated just beneath the skin, though contrary to popular belief the protein is well distributed throughout.

The potato was originally the staple food of the Incas of South America and has been in cultivation for at least 4,000 years.

Potatoes (*Solanum tuberosum*) belong to the same plant family (Solanaceae) as the wild flower henbane (*Hyoscamus niger*), which contains the deadly alkaloids hyoscamine and hyoscine. These were the substances used to murderous effect in 1910 by the notorious Dr Crippen to poison his wife.

For the cook – and gardener – the chief consideration in choosing potatoes is between waxy varieties, which keep their shape when boiled, making them perfect for salads, and floury or 'mealy' potatoes for baking, mashing and frying.

KEEP A WELL-STOCKED STORE CUPBOARD

Every cook needs a selection of basic ingredients to hand, including a range of spices and dried herbs. In addition, it is good to have everything needed on hand to make a meal for unexpected guests. Before every kitchen was equipped with refrigerator and freezer, the store cupboard was even more important than it is today.

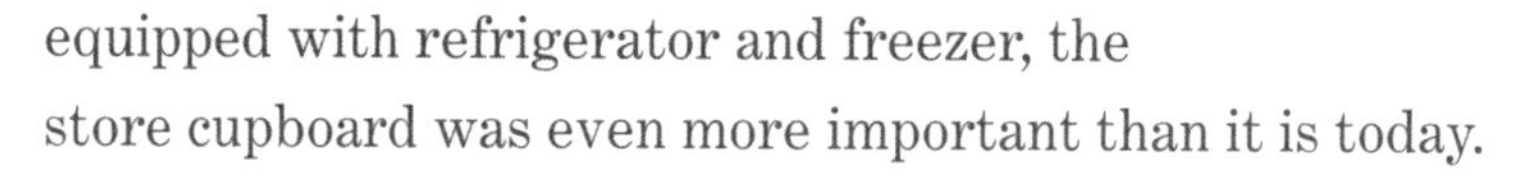

As you add new dishes to your repertoire your range of store cupboard ingredients will build up, among them canned foods, of which tomatoes, pulses and fish such as tuna and anchovies are invaluable. For cakes and desserts add dried fruits and candied peel, as well as flours, sugars, baking powder and bicarbonate of soda. For savoury dishes, bouillon cubes or powder, curry powder, mustard, oils, vinegars and a range of sauces from horseradish to Worcestershire are all handy.

Advising readers on the store cupboard, *Teach Yourself to Cook* of 1946 states that: 'A well-aired cupboard should be available for storage of foodstuffs in constant use. This should be examined daily and cleaned out at frequent intervals.' For storage, it says, 'Ordinary screw-top jars are excellent, or ordinary jam jars can be used and metal lids bought to fit.' Among the many items it lists are a few that are virtually unheard of today, including 'Blanc-mange Powders; Tapioca; Ratafia and Violet Essences; Coralline pepper; Bottled Fruits; and Meat Jelly.'

Mrs Beeton wrote: 'Rice, and all sorts of seed for puddings, should be closely covered to preserve them from insects; but even this will not prevent them from being affected by these destroyers, if they are long and carelessly kept.'

Eat oysters only when there's an 'R' in the month

A catchy way of warning against possible food poisoning from oysters, mussels and other crustaceans in the warmest months of May to August, none of which includes the letter 'r'. Nowadays oysters are bred and farmed to reduce the risk of infection all year round, but in summer, when they are fertile, they have an inferior taste.

Oysters feed on microscopic algae, which can in turn become infected with bacteria that multiply rapidly in warm sea water. Of these, *Vibrio parahaemolyticus* is the most common, causing stomach pains and sickness, but most deadly is *V. vulnificus*, which can bring on septicaemia. What's more, one bad oyster can sensitize you to all others.

A 'good' oyster should always be tightly closed, opening when it is cooked. If it is to be eaten raw, an oyster must be scrubbed clean then prized open with an oyster knife. Cooks would traditionally keep live oysters in

'He was a very valiant man who first adventured on eating oysters.' (Thomas Fuller)

the kitchen and feed them with oatmeal for a few days to fatten them and make them more luscious. The smallest were saved for eating raw; larger ones were cooked and added to steak pies or turkey stuffing, made into patties or dipped in batter and fried. Oysters were so abundant in England in the early 19th century that they were poor people's food. Sam Weller, in Charles Dickens' *Pickwick Papers,* declares that 'poverty and oysters always seem to go together'. They were also exported. In *Sketches by Boz* Dickens describes an oyster shop with 'natives laid, one deep, in circular marble basins in the windows, together with little round barrels of oysters directed to Lords and Baronets, and Colonels and Captains, in every part of the habitable globe.'

The reputation of oysters as an aphrodisiac (the famed 18th-century Italian lover Casanova is said to have eaten 40 oysters a day) may be justified by their mineral content as well as their looks and texture. They are rich in zinc, a substance essential to sperm production.

OYSTER DISHES

Hangtown Fry – an American dish is said to have been the favourite 'last breakfast' in Placerville, California, a settlement nicknamed Hangtown in 1849 from its overzealous judge. It is an omelette made with oysters dipped in egg and flour or breadcrumbs and fried.

Carpetbag steak – a grilled steak stuffed with oysters. So named, it became most popular in Australia in the 1950s, but the combination was commonplace in 19th-century cookbooks.

Oysters Rockefeller – made using oysters, spinach, parsley, onions and breadcrumbs. The colour of the finished dish (the same as that of greenbacks) was significant because it was 'rich as Rockefeller'. The original recipe, devised by Antoine Alciatore of Antoine's in New Orleans, remains a secret.

Dried mushrooms are very useful when fresh ones are not to be had

A useful tip, despite the fact that fresh cultivated mushrooms can now be had all the year round. Dried mushrooms have an intense flavour capable of transforming a risotto, soup or casserole. For country dwellers able to collect wild mushrooms, drying is a better way of dealing with a bumper harvest than freezing.

For the best flavour you need superior mushrooms, which is why dried ceps are hard to match.

To dry mushrooms Richard Dolby in his 1833 *Cook's Dictionary* provides this method: 'Wipe them quite clean, and take out the brown, and pare off the skin of the large ones; lay them on paper, and put them in a cool oven to dry, keep them in paper bags in a very dry place. When wanted for use, simmer them in gravy, and they will swell to nearly their former size.' After drying, mushrooms may be ground to a powder and stored in airtight bottles.

Another way of using a flush of mushrooms is to convert them into ketchup, an ingredient that will add flavour to any savoury dish. For this, mushrooms are salted and left to stand for 12 days. The liquor is then strained off, boiled with black pepper, mace, ginger, a few cloves and mustard seed and bottled. The ketchup does, however, need to be used within three months or, if not, reboiled to sterilize it. Better yet is a quintessence of mushrooms, a delicate relish obtained by sprinkling mushrooms with a little salt, then, after three hours, mashing them with a fork. The following day, says Dolby, 'strain off the liquor that will flow from them, and boil it in a stewpan until reduced to half. It will not keep long, but is delicate in flavour.'

REJECT ANY MUSSEL THAT DOES NOT OPEN

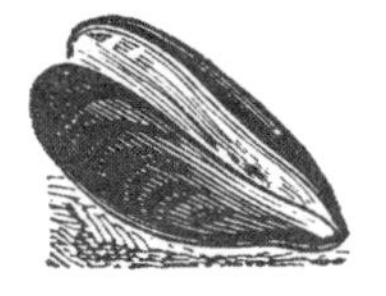

An extremely wise precaution – a mussel that fails to open when it is cooked is most likely to be bad. And before cooking, any mussels that have chipped or broken shells, or that do not close when tapped sharply, should also be discarded. Mussels are excellent served with French bread or, in the Belgian tradition, with *frîtes* (fries).

Fishermen are superstitious about throwing empty mussel shells into the sea in case they attract bad weather.

Preparing mussels is a chore, but worth the effort for any shellfish lover. They need to be well scrubbed under running water and all barnacles and pieces of seaweed scraped off with a small knife. For *moules marinière* all you need do is bring to the boil in a large pan some white wine with parsley stalks, garlic and shallots added, put in the mussels, cover the pan and shake them over a high heat for a few minutes until they open. The parsley leaves are chopped and sprinkled over the mussels. The assiduous cook will strain the cooking liquid through muslin before serving to remove any grit, sand or pieces of shell.

Billi-bi soup, a broth made with mussels, then thickened with cream and egg yolks and served topped with Parmesan cheese, was created in the 1920s, probably by Louis Barthe at Ciro's restaurant in Deauville for an American client named William Brand ('Billy B.'). In Italy, the big, fat mussels of the Mare Piccolo, a saltwater lagoon in Puglia, are made into the dish *teglia di cozze*, in which they are baked in combination with potatoes, courgettes (zucchini) and tomatoes.

Mussels are widely produced from 'mussel seeds' or larvae, which are grown in protected areas or 'lays'. These nutrient-rich waters are kept clean and free of mud until the mussels are large enough to be harvested at two to three years of age.

MUSSEL POWER

Worldwide, there are many types of edible mussels, all delicious. Horse mussels, however, are inferior in quality.

Common mussel – *Mytilus edulis* – dark blue shells, harvested wild but also farmed. Found all over the northern hemisphere.

Green-lipped mussel – *Perna canaliculus* – native of New Zealand, also found in Australian waters. Brown shells with green lips.

Bearded mussel – *Modiolus barbatus* – typified by its prominent beard, also called the horse mussel.

Asian green mussel – *Perna viridis* – has a greenish black shell. Widely used in Asian cuisine with flavourings such as lemon grass and coriander.

BOIL A SOFT EGG FOR FOUR MINUTES

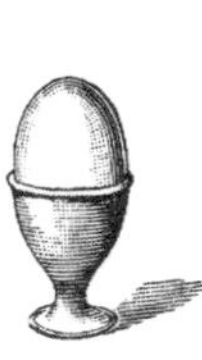

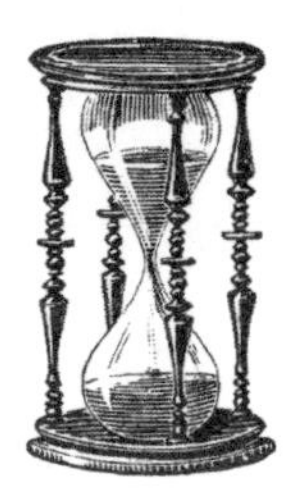

A hard one for ten minutes, at least. It sounds easy, but it is quite a skill to boil an egg so that it is perfectly cooked.

As Eliza Acton says of egg boiling, 'Even this simple process demands a certain degree of care for if the eggs be brought from a cold larder, and suddenly plunged into boiling water they will frequently break immediately, and a large portion will often escape from their shells. In winter they

When a boiled egg is eaten it is said to be unlucky to break it open at the small or narrow end.

Putting eggs into boiling water, not cold, helps to avoid the formation of dark rings between white and yolk when they are hard boiled.

should be held over the steam for an instant before they are laid in, and they should be put in gently. They should be put into sufficient boiling water to cover them completely.' The timings Miss Acton recommends are:

Three minutes 'for people who like the whites in a partially liquid state'.
Three and a half minutes for whites cooked 'to a milky consistency'.
Four to four and a half minutes 'not a second more', which will 'cook the whites firm but leave the yellow liquid'.
Eight to ten minutes for hard boiled but 'for a salad dressing, 15 minutes'.

To save energy the Acton way, put an egg in a basin, pour over boiling water to cover it completely, put a plate over the basin and leave it for 12 minutes. The egg will be 'perfectly and beautifully cooked'.

HARD-BOILED DELICACIES

Some favourite old-time ways with hard-boiled eggs from the country kitchen:

Convent eggs – rings of egg in onion sauce, served on toast.

Scalloped eggs – finely chopped hard-boiled eggs mixed with flour, chopped parsley, minced ham and cream, formed into balls then dipped into egg, then fine breadcrumbs and fried.

Scotch eggs – whole hard-boiled eggs enclosed in sausagemeat, dipped in egg and breadcrumbs and fried.

Egg pie – a mixture of chopped hard-boiled egg, suet, currants and cream, seasoned with nutmeg and cinnamon and baked.

Never test caramel with your finger

Because it is, of course, extremely hot, and you risk a serious burn. A sugar thermometer is much safer, but experienced cooks prefer to use their eyes to judge when caramel is just right. You also need to be very careful when adding water to hot caramel as it can spit viciously and dangerously.

To make caramel for a caramel crème dessert, you need to heat 175g (6oz) caster sugar in a metal pan over medium heat. Watch it all the time until the sugar begins to melt and is just turning liquid around the edges. Shake the pan, then return it to the heat until about a quarter of the sugar has melted. Using a wooden spoon, stir gently and carry on cooking for 10–15 minutes until the sugar is liquid and a deep brown (on a sugar thermometer this will be about 154°C/310°F). Off the heat, and with your hand covered with a tea towel, add two tablespoons of water. The liquid caramel can then be poured into the bottom of a mould and a custard mixture added.

For a crème brûlée, sugar is heated on top of the rich cream dessert to make a hard caramel, with the sugar being heated under the grill or, by modern cooks, with a blow torch. The old-fashioned way of caramelizing the sugar was with a salamander, an iron disk at the end of an iron rod, which was heated until red hot then passed over the top of the dish. The recipe first appeared in 1691 in the cookbook by the French chef François Massialot, but Trinity College in Cambridge also

The word 'caramel' was first recorded in French cookery in the 17th century. It apparently arrived from Portugal, via Spain, from a word for both an elongated loaf of sugar and an icicle, possibly because they were both shiny and similar in shape. The root of the Portuguese word is the Greek *kalamos*, 'straw', which may refer to its colour.

lays claim to its origins under the name 'Cambridge Burnt Cream' or 'Trinity Cream'. Certainly the college kitchen has a branding iron with the official college crest on it, which is used to burn the sugar top.

Add fresh herbs at the end of cooking, dried at the beginning

An assured route to good flavour, but not advice to follow slavishly. For dishes such as casseroles a *bouquet garni* of fresh parsley, rosemary and thyme added to the pot at the beginning of cooking is needed to give both depth and subtlety of taste.

The specific aromatic notes of herbs – created from a whole spectrum of chemicals released when the leaves are crushed or heated – make them perfect partners for certain ingredients: mint or rosemary with lamb; fennel or dill with fish; bay with ham; sage with pork; tarragon with eggs. Fresh coriander comes into its own in chilli-based Thai curries.

Like rosemary and thyme, bay and sage have sturdy leaves that will impart flavour throughout the cooking of a dish. Herbs with more tender foliage, including fresh coriander (cilantro), chives, dill, fennel, basil, mint and tarragon, are best kept until shortly before the end of cooking for their flavour to be fully appreciated (as is fresh parsley if you want its flavour to be dominant, as in parsley sauce) because when cooked for more than a few minutes their taste goes flat.

Equally, none of these delicate herbs holds its aroma well when dried, though they freeze well (ice cube trays make excellent containers). Or try making good quantities of garden mint into sauce or jelly, and turn fresh basil into your own pesto, which will keep for at least a month in the refrigerator.

THE VALUE OF HERBS

Herbs were used for medicinal purposes long before they became part of the cook's everyday armoury, and many have strong associations with myths and superstitions:

Bay – a healer and protector. Bay is the symbol of victory and honour. The sudden death of a bay tree is said to foretell pestilence or the death of kings.

Sage – as long as sage prospers in a man's garden so too, it is said, will his business.

Basil – said to be the antidote to a scorpion sting and a herb to protect a household.

Rosemary – protects the house near which it is grown. It is thrown into a grave to symbolize remembrance of the dead.

Mint – the cure-all of the 17th century, used to treat everything from colic to venereal disease.

Parsley – the herb a woman should pick when she wants to have a baby. Parsley stalks will freshen the breath when chewed.

DON'T LET A PUDDING BOIL TOO FAST

Gently simmering water is all a steamed or boiled pudding needs to keep it at a steady temperature. The prudent cook will also regularly check the level of water in the pan and top it up with boiling water from a kettle as necessary.

That the 'proof of the pudding is in the eating' means that the true test of something is in its performance, not its promise.

Steamed puddings are best cooked in the top section of a steamer, which is a two-sectioned pan, the halves separated by a perforated plate. Robust puddings can be cooked in an ordinary saucepan with some boiling water in the base. 'A pudding which is to be boiled,' *The Skilful Cook* of 1919 explains, 'should be placed in a well-greased basin or mould, which it should quite fill.' Some suet puddings, it adds, 'may be cooked without the basin . . . When cooked in this way it is well to put a plate in the saucepan to prevent the pudding sticking to the bottom and burning.'

Today's cook will cover a pudding made in a basin with two pieces of greaseproof paper, placed at right angles, each with a pleat in the centre to allow for expansion as the pudding rises. The whole is then covered with foil, similarly placed and pleated. The cook of old would use a scalded, floured cloth, with room allowed for swelling, but whatever the covering it needs to be tied on securely and a 'handle' made with the string to enable the basin to be removed from the pan with ease. Another tip for easy lifting out is to place strips of cloth under the basin, long enough to hang over the sides of the pan.

PUDDINGS GALORE

Boiled and steamed puddings are the ultimate in comfort food, and many have names that immediately evoke bygone nursery days. Custard is the traditional accompaniment.

Spotted Dick – a sweet sponge or suet mixture with a generous addition of currants.

Apple hat – a suet crust filled with chopped cooking apples and sugar.

Cabinet pudding – a bowl lined with sponge fingers (lady fingers) then filled with a vanilla flavoured egg custard mixture. The bowl may also be decorated with a few raisins or cherries.

Jam roly poly – suet pastry rolled out, spread with jam then rolled up and boiled in a cloth. The roly poly may also be filled with syrup, mincemeat or apples, alone or mixed with dates or raisins.

Sussex pond pudding – suet pastry used to line a basin into which is put sugar, butter and a whole lemon. When the pudding is served a 'pond' of lemony, buttery sauce runs out.

Roxane pudding – a very light steamed sponge with beaten egg whites folded into the mixture. Served with a lemon or chocolate sauce.

Marmalade pudding – a suet and breadcrumb mixture with eggs and marmalade added, served with a marmalade sauce.

WASH VEGETABLES IN THREE WATERS

Whenever vegetables come straight from the garden or allotment they need plenty of washing to free them of 'natural' dirt from the ground. Supermarket vegetables – even those sold pre-washed – still benefit from thorough cleaning to help rid them of pesticides or other chemicals used in their growing.

One of the great pleasures of life is to eat peas fresh from the pod. Naturally shielded from dirt, they need no pre-washing.

Fresh spinach leaves seem especially attractive to grit, and three washes may well be needed to get them clean. Cabbage can also be earthy, and when home grown can harbour the green caterpillars of the cabbage white butterfly. Leeks trap dirt between the layers of leaves in each tightly packed cylinder. Slicing downwards through the leek in two cuts made at right angles to each other frees the upper parts of the leaves so that they can be washed under running water. Carrots and parsnips are best washed then scraped, not peeled, unless they are extremely dirty. Peeling robs them of their complete flavour.

When food was scarce in wartime, cooks would wash badly infested cabbage or cauliflower heads in salt water or soak them in vinegar before cooking to kill any caterpillars rather than putting them on the compost heap or in 'swill' for feeding pigs. Cooks of the 1920s were advised that, before washing vegetables, they should 'give them a little slap against the palm of the hand, and much of the dirt, sand and insects will drop off which would otherwise stick when plunged into the water'.

Keep meringues in the airing cupboard

A good way of ensuring that meringue dries out and stays crisp, but not the way to treat soft meringue. Success with meringues lies in the beating and in choosing the correct temperature for cooking. Meringue baskets cooked in advance of when you need them will indeed keep perfectly in airtight tins for several months in the warmth of the airing cupboard.

For whisking up all meringues a grease-free bowl, ideally of copper (see page 91) or alternatively of glass, china or steel, is essential. The basic proportions are 50g (2oz) caster sugar to each egg white. First the whites are beaten until stiff with a balloon or electric whisk, then half the sugar is added and the mixture beaten again until it is smooth and has a satiny sheen. The remaining sugar is then folded in. To make small, crisp meringues, spoonfuls of the mixture are placed on greaseproof paper or non-stick baking parchment and cooked for 2½–3 hours at 110°C/225°F/Gas ¼.

Richard Dolby in his 1833 *Cook's Dictionary* describes a finish popular at the time and still a superb way to serve meringues: '. . . when quite crisp take them out, turn them over with the paper, and take out some of the middle very gently with a spoon and put them in the oven to dry, and bake that side. Keep in a dry place until wanted, then fill them with whipt cream well flavoured, or something acid; stick two together to form the egg . . . Occasionally,' he adds, 'they may be coloured red for a change.'

Soft meringue is used to top a lemon meringue pie or similar dessert. Agnes Marshall's 'Fleur with Meringue' was a custard tart topped with meringue and fresh fruit. Maria Parloa, in her *Kitchen Companion* of 1887, includes a strawberry meringue pudding. First a meringue is made with seven egg whites, seven tablespoons of powdered sugar and half a teaspoon of salt. Beginning with meringue in the base, meringue and preserve are put into a dish in alternate layers and the whole baked in a moderate oven for 25 minutes. 'Serve very cold,' she says, 'with whipped cream.'

For a crisp outside and soft centre, add a little vinegar and cornflour to a meringue mixture.

Both Australia and New Zealand claim to have invented the Pavlova, a shallow meringue basket filled with whipped cream and fresh fruit. The name – and the recipe – began appearing following widely acclaimed tours of New Zealand in 1926 and Australia in 1929 by the Russian prima ballerina Anna Pavlova, although the definitive recipe is thought to have been created in 1935 by chef Herbert Sachse at the Hotel Esplanade in Perth, Australia. Whatever the truth, it is certain that cooks and chefs in both countries sought to honour Pavlova's visits with confections designed to capture her light, airy spirit and performance.

Store vanilla pods in the sugar jar

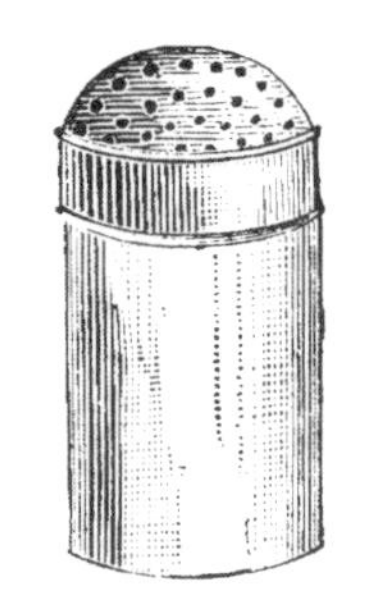

Not only a good way of keeping the pods from drying out, it provides wonderfully flavoured sugar for use in sweet things of all kinds, including cakes, custards and ice creams.

Vanilla pods or beans are the fruits of a type of parasitic orchid native to Central America, which grows as a vine around the trees that are its host. When encountered by the Spaniards in the 15th century, the Emperor Montezuma was observed to drink a concoction of cacao beans and vanilla called *tlilxochitl*. It is said that because the Spanish had difficulty in pronouncing this name they opted for *baynilla* or 'little pod', from which we get the name vanilla. The odour of vanilla was so strong that it was said to intoxicate the men who climbed the trees to pick it.

For kitchen use, vanilla pods picked before they are ripe are plunged into hot steam then left to ferment for up to four weeks. The most intense flavour is found in the seeds, which can be scraped out and used in custards. For a milder flavour the pod can be infused whole, then dried and stored in a jar of sugar until it is needed again.

Never entrust the composition of your mustard to any hand but your own . . .

Sound advice from Launcelot Sturgeon in *The Importance of Good Living* published in 1822, when ready-mixed mustard was unheard of. The popularity of mustard in European cooking owes much to the fact that, unlike more exotic spices, it flourishes in temperate climates.

Sturgeon's command continues '. . . unless you should be fortunate enough to possess a maître d'hotel, or butler, in whom you can place the most implicit confidence: next, let the powder be invariably mixed with champagne in lieu of water; then, add a small quantity of essence of anchovy, and one drop – light as the morning dew upon a rose-bed – of asafoetida [a pungent resin-like gum].'

Mustard is made from the seeds of various plants of the brassica family (see box overleaf), which when crushed and mixed with water release volatile, highly flavoured compounds that attain their peak strength after about ten minutes; they then fade unless they are stabilized with vinegar or some other acid ingredient such as verjuice (wine must). Archaeological remains suggest that mustard was cultivated by the ancients, and it was described as a condiment by the Roman writer Columella in AD 42.

Until the 18th century the only way to prepare mustard was to grind the seeds into an oily paste and mix it by hand, but in 1720 a Mrs Clements of Tewkesbury discovered how to mill the seeds into a dry powder, ready to use. Others soon took up the practice of creating this 'made mustard', among them Keen & Sons in London and, notably, Jeremiah Colman of Norwich, whose mustard powder contained turmeric and wheat flour to improve the texture of the mixture of ground black and white mustard seeds.

Mustard is the ideal accompaniment to everything from roast beef to frankfurters. In Italy it is used in *mostarda di frutta*, a fruit preserve containing cherries, oranges, plums and figs and honey, flavoured with mustard oil. Rather like a sweet chutney, this is eaten with hot and cold meats.

KNOW YOUR MUSTARDS

Mustard seeds come from several plant species; both these and the way mustard is mixed are crucial to its flavour:

White – seeds of *Sinapis alba*, also known as yellow mustard.

Black – seeds of *Brassica nigra*, common in Asia but now grown as a spice and no longer included in mustard powder.

Brown or Chinese – seeds of *Brassica juncea*, widely grown in both Europe and Asia.

English – a strong mustard made from white mustard seeds.

Bordeaux – a mild mustard with sugar and (usually) tarragon added.

Dijon – mild mustard traditionally mixed with verjuice.

Meaux – a mild mustard containing quantities of uncrushed grains.

Parsley makes a universal garnish

By far the most popular way of adding colour to a dish, parsley is also excellent deep fried or crisped in the oven. For decoration, the curly-leaved type looks best, but as an ingredient most cooks prefer flat-leaved parsley because, when young, its foliage has more depth of flavour. A parsley sauce is a perfect accompaniment to ham, fish and vegetables such as broad beans and carrots.

Parsley has been used medicinally for many generations to cure everything from bad breath and dyspepsia to swellings of the eyes and the pain of earache.

The green, woody and distinctive flavour of parsley, which grows wild in southern Europe, has been appreciated since ancient times. The Greeks called both parsley and celery, to which it is closely related, *selinon*, but they gave parsley the distinguishing name of *petroselinon* or 'rock celery'. As well as cooking it, they used it to crown the heads of victors at their Isthmian games and to adorn the tombs of the dead. The Romans seem to have used both curly and flat-leaved parsley, and in the 8th century the Emperor Charlemagne also commended its flavour.

A crisp parsley garnish is both decorative and delicious. It can be deep fried for 15 seconds in hot fat, then drained, or as Miss T. M. Hope describes in her *Young Woman's Companion* of 1811: 'When you have picked and washed your parsley quite clean, put it in a Dutch oven, or on a sheet of paper. Set it at a moderate distance from the fire, and keep turning until it is quite crisp.

Lay little bits of butter on it, but not to make it greasy. This is a much better method than that of frying.'

Parsley reached Britain in the 16th century and quickly became popular. A béchamel sauce with parsley added is a British favourite of long standing and was enjoyed by Henry VIII. Another way of making a sauce was to boil parsley stalks in water or stock and use this, after straining, as the liquid for adding to a roux made with flour and bacon fat. The chopped leaves of curled parsley, plus a spoonful of cream, are added to complete the sauce. For the French, a *persillade*, a mixture of chopped parsley and garlic, is added to a dish at the end of cooking. In Italian cuisine it is a key ingredient – with capers and chopped cornichons – of the green sauce *salsa verde*.

PARSLEY WISE

Of all herbs, parsley is among the richest in related superstitions and sayings:

Parsley seeds are notoriously slow to germinate, and it is said that they take so long because they have to visit the devil before the leaves will emerge.

Where parsley grows faster, the mistress is master – that is, the woman rules the roost.

To avoid bad luck, never transplant parsley or give away parsley plants.

A young woman wanting to get pregnant should plant parsley seeds.

It is said that baby boys come from under nettles, baby girls from the parsley bed.

TEST AN EGG FOR FRESHNESS BY PUTTING IT IN WATER

In cold water, a fresh egg will sink and lie level on the bottom of a bowl; a stale or bad one – in which gas has accumulated – will float. This sure-fire test was first recorded by the English cook Hannah Glasse, the first 'celebrity chef', in 1750.

'. . . an egg which has succeeded in being fresh has done all that can be reasonably expected of it.' (Henry James)

Another less reliable test is to hold the egg up to a bright light. The shell will be almost transparent and it will be possible to see both the yolk and an unclouded white. A stale egg is more transparent at the ends than in the middle. In a fresh egg the reverse is true.

The key to these simple tests is that an egg begins to change as soon as it leaves the hen's body because it continues to 'breathe', releasing carbon dioxide gas. Gradually, the white and yolk change, too. The white becomes thinner and the membrane or sac around the yolk weakens, making it more difficult for the cook to separate white and yolk without the yolk breaking. Eventually the egg rots, producing smelly hydrogen sulphide from the yolk.

Eggs have been used to celebrate Easter since the 12th century, when they were cooked in water with cochineal added: the red colour symbolized the blood of Christ. But long before this the ancient Greeks gave each other gifts of painted eggs to celebrate the arrival of spring.

Even a fresh egg can harbour *Salmonella* food poisoning bacteria passed on by the hen. To avoid the risk of infection, which can be dangerous to the young, the pregnant, the elderly and infirm, they should avoid raw eggs and cook them until the yolk is completely set.

Every cook should prepare her own pickles

Pickles are great store cupboard ingredients, and perfect accompaniments to cheese, cold meats and meat pies. Before the days of the deep freeze, pickling was one of the key ways of preserving vegetables for winter use. To be enjoyed at their best, pickles need time for their flavours to mature.

Whatever the ingredients – whether onions, cabbage, walnuts, gherkins or a mixture of vegetables – vinegar and salt are key ingredients in pickling; both of them act to kill bacteria and prevent decay by moulds. Fruits such as peaches and pears also make good pickles, with sugar and cinnamon added to the vinegar.

The oldest of all Europe's pickles is sauerkraut, made by layering cabbage leaves with salt and leaving them to ferment. In his *Shilling Cookery for the People* of 1854 Alexis Soyer gives his recommendations for red cabbage: 'Cut them into thin slices, remove the hard stalk, lay them on a slab, cover them with salt for twelve hours turning them now and then, clean off all the salt and place them in stone jars; boil some vinegar, and to every quart add one ounce of black pepper, and seven button onions, or two large ones, sliced, boil for five minutes, and pour it over cabbage; cover the jar, and let it remain three weeks before using.'

The pickled onion has been known since at least 1740, when Hannah Glasse provided her readers with a recipe for preserving small onions in spiced brine. In the following century Eliza Acton recommended using white wine vinegar and Reading onions, a variety no longer available. For the modern cook, shallots are an excellent substitute, or small silverskin onions grown specifically for pickling.

Pickled walnuts are a British speciality and an 'esteemed condiment' that became highly fashionable in the 18th century. The nuts, still green and before the shell forms, were picked at midsummer and steeped in brine for between 9 and 42 days before being drained, exposed to sunlight for two or three days, then added to spiced vinegar. This method had the advantage that it used the nuts while green: except in a hot summer walnuts can be reluctant to ripen.

Some editions of Hannah Glasse's Art of Cookery *include a recipe for a ginger-flavoured pickle called 'paco lilla'.*

Piccallilli, a mixed mustard pickle of cauliflower, beans, cucumber and onions, is renowned for its vivid yellow colour, produced by the spice turmeric. It has been known since the 18th century but its heat and sharpness means that it is not to everyone's taste. In *Kettner's Book of the Table* of 1877 the author E. S. Dallas writes: 'The best mixed pickles, even those of the great magicians of Soho, Crosse and Blackwell, are now made with a woebegone compound called Piccallilli. The good old sort is neglected . . .'

Bread-and-butter pickles, favourites in America, are mixed pickles of cucumber and onions with vinegar, sugar, mustard and celery seeds. As their name suggests, they are excellent in sandwiches.

Never touch curry powder with a wooden spoon

Good advice, unless you keep a spoon specifically for curries, as the wood will absorb the curry flavours and may impart them to the next dish you stir, which could be a delicate sweet custard.

After natural scoops such as sea shells, empty gourd skins and coconuts, wood was one of the earliest materials used for spoons, along with animal horn.

Stir any mixture containing butter, cream or other dairy produce with a wooden spoon that you have used for curry or any other savoury dish and you risk passing on an unpleasant taste, even if the spoon was thoroughly washed after its previous use. Curry, especially if it contains the vivid yellow spice turmeric, will also indelibly stain a wooden spoon.

The well-equipped cook will have different wooden spoons for sweet and savoury dishes, and a selection of spoons in different sizes for different kitchen tasks. A small 'corner spoon', whose bowl is drawn to a point on one side, is ideal for getting into every inch of a pan when stirring a sauce. Another way of creating the same sort of shape is to use – and wear down – the same wooden spoon for 30 years.

Curry began as a spicy soup-like sauce to accompany rice – the Tamil *kari* – but by the 16th century the English word had become a catch-all for anything cooked in such a sauce. Although spice mixes are freshly prepared for each dish in India, British cooks sought a ready-made alternative, and curry powder was first sold in Britain in the late 1700s. The first curry recipe to appear in English was Hannah Glasse's 'How to Make Curry the India Way', published in 1747. In it, meat and rice were cooked together with the addition of various spices.

Heat a lemon before you squeeze it

An old cook's trick, made even easier if you have a microwave. Just 30 seconds on 'high' will soften the fruit's internal membranes. Five minutes in a warm oven works equally well. When buying lemons, a good tip is to judge them by their weight, not their looks – for their size they should feel heavy in the hand.

Lemon juice is one of the cook's essential ingredients, for everything from a marinade to tenderize meat to a flavouring for a cake, so it makes sense to get every last drop of juice from the fruit. As an alternative to gentle heat, another good way to help release the maximum juice from a lemon (or lime) is to roll it backwards and forwards on a work surface a few times before squeezing it.

Old-fashioned mechanical lemon squeezers come in two basic designs – the hand-held wooden 'reamer' and the glass pyramid moulded in a dish to catch the juice with protrusions to trap pips and pulp. One ingenious 1930s device for extracting juice when just a few drops were needed consisted of a perforated aluminium tube that was pushed into the lemon before the fruit was gently squeezed.

Lemons were an expensive rarity until the 16th century, when the Italians began growing them in quantity and the Spanish planted the first lemon groves in California. When this rich lemon cheesecake recipe was written in the 1740s in the *Compleat Housewife of Williamsburg, Virginia*, lemons would still have been a great luxury: 'Take two large lemons, grate off the peel of both and squeeze out the juice of one; add it to half a pound of fine sugar; twelve yolks of eggs, eight egg whites well beaten; then melt half a pound of butter in four or five spoonfuls of cream; then stir it all together, and set it over the fire, stirring 'till it be pretty thick . . . when 'tis cold, fill your patty-pans little more than half full; put a fine paste very thin at the bottom . . . half a hour, with a quick oven, will bake them.'

Save time and energy with a pressure cooker

Undoubtedly a useful addition to the battery of cooking utensils for dishes that would otherwise be boiled or steamed, since the high temperature at which food cooks tenderizes meat, preserves nutrients and cuts cooking time.

The original pressure cooker was created in the 1680s by the French physicist, mathematician and inventor Denis Papin. He made a large cast iron vessel with a lid that locked, so trapping in the steam and raising the cooking temperature inside to 15 per cent above boiling. This early version, called a 'steam digester', was difficult to regulate, however, and explosions were common.

It took several more centuries for pressure cookers to reach the kitchen; the first commercial ones, made by National Presto Industries, went on show in 1939 at the New York World Fair. Since then, designs have gradually been improved, but even today's high-tech models have the disadvantage that unless food is browned beforehand it is apt to taste bland and lack deep flavour.

An old-fashioned way of saving energy was with a cooking or hay box. Essentially a tea chest or other large box lined with newspaper and filled with hay or straw, it was used to cook a dish that nested inside it, thoroughly insulated, over a period of six hours or more. The only pre-cooking necessary was to bring the dish to the boil. Extolling its virtues of 'saving coal, saving time, and saving money', *Girl Guiding* of 1929 declared it 'jolly useful' and invaluable at camp.

The slow cooker, an electric version of the hay box, arrived in the 1970s. As with a pressure cooker, if it is to have a good flavour the food needs browning ahead of cooking and also generous seasoning.

Keep your lids on

The best way of saving energy when using saucepans, unless you need to stir a mixture continuously. With the lid on you can keep the contents at boiling point with the hob at a much lower temperature and also prevent unnecessary evaporation.

The cooking pot itself is much older than the lid – the first pots to have lids were called kettles, and their use spread across Europe with Roman culture and cookery in the 1st century AD.

Writing on 'kitchen furnishing' in 1887, Maria Parloa advised against iron pans 'of poor quality'. She recommended those 'with either porcelain or tin lining' which only needed washing in soap and water and did not have to be oiled after washing up to stop them from rusting. These she rightly declared especially good for long slow cooking 'because the article cooking can be kept at a more even temperature'.

'As not only health but life may be said to depend on the cleanliness of culinary utensils, great attention must be paid to their condition generally, but more especially to that of the saucepans, stewpans and boilers.' (Mrs Beeton)

Every cook needs a good range of pans with well-fitting lids. Six pans of different sizes and depths – one of them lidless and lipped for good pouring – will be enough for most jobs. A frying pan with a lid is also useful for tasks such as poaching fish and fruit. Stainless steel is the best material and far superior to the aluminium and tinned metal used by previous generations. High quality tin-lined copper remains top notch if you have the time and energy to look after it.

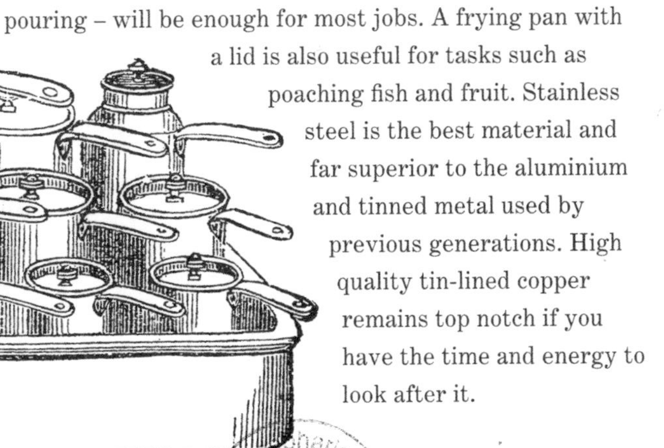

INDEX